CHRISTIAN LEADERS
OF THE SEVENTEENTH CENTURY

BY *J.C. Ryle*

EDITED & INTRODUCED BY LEE GATISS

Christian Leaders of the Seventeenth Century
by J. C. Ryle

© Church Society/Lost Coin Books, 2015.

Published for Church Society by Lost Coin Books, London.
email: lostcoinbooks@gmail.com
web: www.lostcoinbooks.com

LOST COIN

Church Society
Tel: +44 (0) 1923-235111
www.churchsociety.org
admin@churchsociety.org

Church Society, Ground Floor, Centre Block
Hille Business Estate, 132 St Alban's Road
Watford WD24 4AE, UK
Tel +44 (0)1923 255410

ISBN: 9781784980344

Printed in the UK

What people are saying about this book

This publication of Ryle's analysis of Christian leaders of the past is a timely reminder for Christian leaders of the present. My introduction to JC Ryle was in my teens when I first read *Knots Untied*. I had been exploring some of the difficult questions that many Anglicans face and Bishop Ryle's analysis I found refreshing and convincing, even though he had written nearly 100 years ago. I began to read as much of Ryle as I could find, and I am therefore delighted to commend this publication.

Glenn Davies, Archbishop of Sydney

Bishop Ryle is the only nineteenth-century Anglican divine whose works are still in print and enjoyed by people all over the world. Some of his writings are scattered and hard to find, which makes this collection particularly valuable. Ryle speaks to our situation with a clarity that few have equalled, and his voice needs to be heard as much now as when these chapters were first produced.

Gerald Bray, Editor of Churchman

I am grateful to Lee Gatiss for re-introducing JC Ryle to modern Church people, and in particular for making available this new collection. Ryle provides a clear and compelling vision for a truly Protestant and Evangelical Church of England to flourish today. He believed that every generation needed to own its Reformed heritage and, to that end, I am grateful that this volume has been put into our hands now.

Simon Vibert, Vice Principal of Wycliffe Hall, Oxford

I love J C Ryle! Of all the bishops we have had since the good bishops of the Reformation period, he is the most loved and widely respected, and his writings have done, and continue to do, so much good for the gospel cause. Once again we are indebted to Lee Gatiss for this excellent collection. May Ryle be rediscovered and enjoyed by a new generation! And may we, please God, have a fresh injection of Ryle's clarity and courage!

Wallace Benn, former President of the Church of England Evangelical Council

JC Ryle speaks in this book of "the immense importance of the laity taking timely interest in the condition of the Church of England." I am therefore delighted to commend this excellent collection of his historical writings, which will help all laity understand why the Church of England is worth fighting for, and why we have to be part of the fight."

**Debbie Woods, Associate Professor,
University of Law, Manchester.**

Contents

JC Ryle on the Seventeenth Century
Lee Gatiss 7

1. Richard Baxter 23
2. Archbishop Laud 55
3. Samuel Ward 91
4. William Gurnall 111
5. James II and the Seven Bishops 165

JC Ryle on the Seventeenth Century

It was while he was a young incumbent at Helmingham in Suffolk (1844-1861) that Ryle energetically took up writing. This was his third parish, but only then could he afford the books he needed to do his research and the time he needed to compose his thoughts. There for the first time he was paid a full and decent stipend, and with all his parishioners living close by, pastoral visiting was made far easier than it had been for him before.[1] Or as he put it,

> My work in the parish was very simple. There was neither village street, public house, beer shop nor shop of any description. To visit 300 people within a mile of the church on every side was of course very easy work and I had plenty of spare time... there really was very little to be done, and I had more time for reading and thinking and storing my mind than I have ever had before or since.[2]

It is easy to see why despite enjoying regular trips to the capital, he was not easily tempted away from Helmingham.[3] The chapter in this book

---

1 See E. Russell, *That Man of Granite with the Heart of a Child: A New Biography of JC Ryle* (Fearn, Ross-shire: Christian Focus, 2001), 44-47.

2 Peter Toon (ed.), *J.C. Ryle: A Self Portrait. A Partial Autobiography* (Swengel, PA.: Reiner Publications, 1975), page 71.

3 As he says in his biography of Ward, *"it is vain to suppose that the reputation of a preacher, however eminent, who lives and dies in a provincial town, will long survive him. In order to become the subject of biographies, and have the facts of his life continually noted down, a man must live in a metropolis."* Yet in his autobiography (page 80), he remarks on how he *"never liked London as*

7

on Richard Baxter dates from this time and was one of his earliest tracts. It was first published in 1854 alongside studies of the sixteenth-century bishop, Hugh Latimer and the eighteenth-century preacher, George Whitefield. Those other mini-biographies have been republished more recently by the Banner of Truth, in their collections *Five English Reformers* and *Christian Leaders of the Eighteenth Century*. Yet Ryle's work on the seventeenth century and its great heroes and villains is less well-known in our day, until now.

Ryle on the Puritans

He was not the type of fundamentalist evangelical who denigrates all study except Bible study. "For my own part," he declared, "I can only say that I read everything I can get hold of which professes to throw light on my Master's business, and the work of Christ among men."[4] He was also not one of those who dismissed the seventeenth century as a time of arid and dusty divines. He did not consider it to be a barren wasteland for true evangelicals, in comparison to the dynamism of the first flush of Reformation or the awakened enthusiasm of the eighteenth-century Revival. He did not draw a negative contrast between the "sound" Reformers and the "speculative" or "overly-systematic" Puritans. Many have written them all off thus, but only out of basic ignorance and ill-informed prejudice. The great champion of evangelicalism had a very different view:

> Let us settle it down in our minds that for sound doctrine, spirituality, and learning combined, the Puritans stand at the head of English divines. With all their faults, weaknesses, and defects, they alone kept the lamp of pure, Evangelical religion burning in this country in the times of the Stuarts.

---

a ministerial sphere" because although he was in demand there he *"always felt that popularity, as it was called, was a very worthless thing and a very bad thing for a man's soul."*

4 Martyn Lloyd-Jones avers that it is the *duty* of a Christian to learn from church history, basing this injunction on the teaching of the Bible itself. See "Can we learn from history?" in *The Puritans: Their Origins and Successors* (Edinburgh: Banner of Truth, 1987), pages 215-216. It seems strangely narcissistic to me that any Christian should discourage an interest in the history of their spiritual family, as if theirs was the only generation that really counts (Job 12:2).

This may be something of an overstatement—there were many, not normally counted as "Puritans", who also held tenaciously to Reformed theology in this period.[5] But it gives no comfort to those who write off the heirs of the Reformation as unworthy successors to Luther and Calvin. There were all sorts of problems in the church during the age of Baxter and Gurnall, as there are in every generation. There was much apostasy from the gospel, and a moving away from the solid doctrinal and practical foundations of the *Thirty-nine Articles* and the *Book of Common Prayer*. The good bishop writes here of "the suicidal blindness of the Church of England" during the seventeenth century. Yet we owe to that epoch a huge debt of gratitude. "To no times are Englishmen so deeply indebted for their civil and religious liberty as the times in which Baxter lived," says Ryle. Evangelical believers and all lovers of religious freedom ought not to forget what they owe to the Puritans.

Ryle speaks of the crowning folly of the Act of Uniformity of 1662, by which most Puritans were ejected from the Church of England. In his view, "a more impolitic and disgraceful deed never disfigured the annals of a Protestant Church." It was disgraceful because it broke promises made by those in power that they would behave tolerantly towards those now deemed "nonconformists", and allow them to flourish unmolested. It was impolitic because even though Ryle considered the Puritans "wrong and misguided in their judgments" on some points, he thought those who rode roughshod over consciences were "far more wrong and far more misguided." Those who held the reins of power failed to heal the divisions in the church and instead sowed the seeds of schism; they refused to make "wise and timely concessions", which could have made the Church of England far more embracive of evangelicals and therefore much more effective. Is there really nothing in this sort of history from which we can learn today?

---

5 See Stephen Hampton, *Anti-Arminians: The Anglican Reformed Tradition from Charles II to George I* (Oxford: Oxford University Press, 2008), who also berates Ryle for this sort of hyperbole (page 3).

Ryle as biographer

As a biographer, Ryle always has an eye on the salutary lessons he can draw from the history he recounts. He always was, and forever remained, a preacher first and foremost. So he is not always as subtle as he might be in painting the portraits of his protagonists. It is clear from the near hagiographical tone of portions of his biography of Baxter, for example, that he was a particular hero for Ryle, and though he acknowledges that the man had weaknesses, he spends little time unravelling them before us. We do not hear much of Baxter's doctrinal aberrations and leadership *faux pas*. This is a pity, though there is of course much to praise as well. William Laud, on the other hand, is subjected to intense scrutiny as the anti-hero; indeed, one might almost say that the beheaded Archbishop was the quintessential "bad guy" of the piece for Ryle.

Ryle did a great deal of his own research, particularly on those of his subjects who had lived and worked in Suffolk, as he did. He utilised local histories (such as Mackerell's *History of Lynn*) but was assiduous in checking out many of the details for himself, in parish registers and libraries. On a broader scale, he relies to a great extent, as will be seen, on the major standard histories of the period by Gilbert Burnet,[6] Henry Hallam,[7] Charles Knight,[8] Thomas Babington (Lord) Macaulay,[9] Leopold von Ranke,[10] and John Stoughton.[11] Like a so-called Whig historian, he emphasises the rise of constitutional government and religious

---

[6] Gilbert Burnet, *The History of my own Times* (originally 1724 and 1734, but Ryle probably used the updated 6-volume edition of 1833). See also his *A Memorial Offered to Her Royal Highness, the Princess Sophia containing a Delineation of the Constitution and Policy of England* (1815 edition). As well as writing a controversial commentary on the Thirty-nine Articles, Bishop Burnet also published an influential *History of the Reformation of the Church of England* (published 1679, 1681, 1714).

[7] Henry Hallam, *The Constitutional History of England* (First Edition: 1827). Hallam is sometimes called the first Whig historian.

[8] Charles Knight, *The Popular History of England: An Illustrated History of Society and Government from the Earliest Period to our own Times* (8 volumes, 1856-1862).

[9] Lord Macaulay, *The History of England from the Accession of James the Second* (4 volumes, 1848, 1855).

[10] Leopold von Ranke, *A History of England Principally in the Seventeenth Century* (1875).

[11] John Stoughton, *Ecclesiastical History of England* (4 volumes, 1867-1870).

freedom, with a focus on particularly significant saints or "heroes." As Michael Bentley has written of such historians,

> the so-called Whigs were predominantly **Christian**, predominantly **Anglican**, thinkers for whom the **Reformation** supplied the critical theatre of enquiry when considering the origins of modern England. When they wrote about the history of the **English constitution**, as so many of them did, they approached their story from the standpoint of having **Good News** to relate. Sometimes (since many of these authors were bishops or ordained priests) their commentary edged over into direct homily. More often it took the form of eternal breeziness, thankfulness and oblique reference to universal truth.[12]

This is certainly true of Ryle, though he acknowledges in a deliberate allusion to the Prayer Book confession that during the Reformation "Things were left undone that ought to have been done, and done that ought not to have been done." Still, his bracing "eternal breeziness" and thankfulness is quite a contrast to the modern preoccupation with "horrible history" and the primitive barbarism of the past. Bentley says elsewhere that for Whig historians, "If the present required constant division of one's contemporaries into sound men and cads, so did the past, which readily yielded to a search for them."[13] And this too has a certain relevance for Ryle, who was a politicised churchman not merely a disinterested observer. He was capable of subtlety and nuance in his judgment of non-evangelicals, but he was always clear in identifying the enemies of truth.

Yet he was not just a Whig—there is a certain "Toryism" too in his distrust of human nature. No doubt driven by theological considerations, he could not accept the idea of the inexorable progress of sinful humanity towards a supposedly enlightened apex in his own day. He is not unremittingly teleological in his praise for the present. There were problems in the settlement he lived under, which was far from perfect. For him,

---

12 Michael Bentley, *Modern Historiography: An Introduction* (London: Routledge, 1998), page 66.

13 Michael Bentley, *Modernizing England's Past: English Historiography in the Age of Modernism, 1870-1970* (Cambridge: Cambridge University Press, 2006), page 52.

it was not so much a matter of evangelicals or the Church being "on the right side of history"—a Marxist-Leninist conception of historical development, nowadays favoured by the co-called "gay lobby", who see their current cultural cachet as indicative of the inexorable onward march of rational progress. No, in Ryle's understanding of the world, the church was involved in an inevitable and perennial struggle for faithfulness and freedom against the world, the flesh, and the devil.

Broadly speaking, Christians have always written church history as a way of promoting the claims of the church to be an ancient religion (not a recent innovation), the true religion (as opposed to the teachings of heretics), and (through martyrologies) a religion worth suffering for. The Reformation sent confessional historians of all types back to the sources looking for signs of religious continuity, while the Enlightenment encouraged them to write without reference to God as an agent in the whole affair.[14] As a church historian, Ryle seeks to promote the Church of England as part of the true church stretching back to the Apostles and Prophets. He defends evangelicalism as the genius of its foundational documents, rather than cuckoo catholicism. And he sets forth his suffering, struggling, holy heroes as an encouragement and an example in the tumults of today. He aims, echoing von Ranke, to set before his readers "the thing as it is"—not simply the empirically verifiable facts, but the essential and real spiritual nature of what happened.[15] While "every age is immediate to God" and demands its own unique attention, it was also possible to look for universal applications.[16]

---

14 See Lee Gatiss, "Christian History / Church History" in *The Encyclopedia of Christian Education* edited by G. T. Kurian and M. A. Lamport (London: Rowman & Littlefield, 2015), Volume 1, pages 268-269.

15 Von Ranke famously claimed that as a historian he aspired to "show what actually happened" (*wie es eigentlich gewesen*). Whether he quite meant this in the reductionistic way some have taken it, is a controverted point, and he probably means (as Ryle does) that he wanted to discover the inner essence of events or perhaps even the divine hand behind them. See R.J. Evans, *In Defence of History* (London: Granta, 1997), page 17.

16 Another phrase of von Ranke, *jede Epoche ist unmittelbar zu Gott*, "every age is immediate / present to God", rejects the teleological approach to history and gives each moment of history a unique importance regardless of what may have developed from it later.

Ryle's Heroes and Villains

There are some heroes missing from his roll-call. Personally, I might have chosen John Owen over Richard Baxter, included Richard Sibbes instead of Samuel Ward, and not passed over Bunyan. I would be tempted to tell the story of Bishop Davenant and his involvement in the Synod of Dort (1618-1619), while not neglecting the courage of the Seven Bishops under James II. In a survey of the century, the Westminster Assembly surely deserves honourable mention as do the Broadmead Baptists and others who suffered under the iniquitous Clarendon Code. From the many possibilities in a century packed with drama and personalities, Ryle, however, selected the people most inspiring to him.

Baxter is here placed first, not just because I believe that chapter was originally written first, but because Ryle himself outlines in that biography the importance of studying the seventeenth century. We can sense in that chapter the origin of these words too, in Ryle's involvement with the Church Association and other evangelical groups which met at Exeter Hall in London (a forerunner of Church Society, and their conferences), opposed by the anti-Puritans of his day. He says,

> But never let us forget to whom we are indebted for all this liberty of conference and association which we enjoy. Never let us forget that there was a time when informers would have tracked all our steps—when constables and soldiers would have rudely broken up our gatherings at Exeter Hall, and when our proceedings would have entailed upon us pains, penalties, fines, and imprisonments. Never let us forget that the happy and profitable freedom which we enjoy was only won by long continued and intense struggles, by the blood and sufferings of noble-minded men, of whom the world was not worthy; and never forget that the men who won this freedom for us were those much-abused men—the Puritans.

As it happens, the freedom he and others enjoyed to meet at Exeter Hall was won in his day particularly by Lord Shaftesbury. Another stalwart of the Church Association and similar movements, he sought through the

Religious Worship Act (1855) to enable evangelism and Bible teaching to flourish in an age of apathy. "We are living in fearful and exciting times of great and growing unbelief," Shaftesbury told the House of Lords, and "there are in this country five millions of persons wholly without instruction of any kind. Depend upon it those millions will never be invited to the Church by tightening the reins of the ecclesiastical system, for, unless the Church is able to act as a missionary Church, and, by the removal of every restriction upon her free actions, to compete with every denomination, my belief is that her existence as an Established Church will not be of long duration."[17] Ryle and Shaftesbury were at one on this issue, although William Wilberforce's high church son, Bishop Samuel Wilberforce, resisted this innovation of the new Puritans.[18]

Next, we find the cad, the villain, the foremost antagonist in Ryle's account—Archbishop William Laud. According to Ryle, "Laud did more harm to the Church of England than any Churchman that ever lived. He inflicted a wound that will never be healed; he worked mischief that will never be repaired." He lists Laud's "monstrous follies" in the petty war the Archbishop waged against the Puritans, and praises him for his relentless energy (in a barely veiled hint that evangelicals need to work harder for their own cause). He was not as bad as many make out, but he was far more a political churchman than a spiritually-minded one, says Ryle. Yet, all the same, "God forbid that we should judge him!"

Ryle does not go as far as many of Laud's contemporaries did and accuse him of actually trying to negotiate away the independence of the Church of England from Rome. Though he is clear where Laud's policy

---

17 Edwin Hodder, *The Life and Work of the Seventh Earl of Shaftesbury* (Cambridge: Cambridge University Press, 2014), Volume 2, page 519. As it happens, the local Anglican vicar sought to inhibit these meetings at Exeter Hall, happening in his parish, despite the support of the Bishop of London. See G.R. Balleine, *A History of the Evangelical Party in the Church of England* (London: Church Book Room Press, 1951), page 195.

18 J.I. Packer, *Faithfulness and Holiness: The Witness of J.C. Ryle* (Wheaton, IL.: Crossway, 2002), pages 36-37 says that *"Ryle may as truly and justifiably be called a Puritan as he is called an evangelical,"* and that Ryle's purposes, priorities, and principles were the same as those of the Puritans. As Ryle himself says, the Puritans were hated because they were thoroughly Protestant and Evangelical—he clearly thought of their cause and his as almost identical.

was heading in the end—to "un-Protestantize the Church of England." That is why Laud was, "always opposing what he called 'Calvinism.' He would fain have made popular Protestant theology odious by painting the doctrines of grace as inseparable from antinomianism and extreme views of election and reprobation. He knew too well that nothing so damages a theological cause as a cleverly chosen nickname." An old trick, still repeated today. "Sound Evangelical teaching was decried and run down, under the specious name of 'Calvinism,'" says Ryle. It was ever thus.

One of the very valuable lessons Ryle draws from the life of Laud is that great harm may be done to a church by a small but unified minority. Inevitably he applies this lesson to the rise of the Tractarian party in his own day. In his "autobiography" he lamented the "pernicious influence" of Harry Wilberforce, Samuel Wilberforce, and Henry Manning (who was related to Wilberforce by marriage), and how they had turned his own family towards ritualism.[19] "Minorities often prove winners in the long run," he warns, and theological enemies must not be underestimated. How clear that lesson ought to be to us today, when tiny cadres of committed and dedicated activists have hurled churches all over the world into storms of protest in order to prosecute their politically-correct agenda.

Ryle's antidote is to mobilise the laity, "the real hope of the Church of England." He truly believed in the basic Protestantism of the ordinary people of England, which was being led astray by influential elites that could only be resisted if the masses were mobilised. As he put it,

> The bulk of our middle classes and educated lower orders in the Church do not want chasubles, copes, dalmatics, birettas, banners, processions, incense, pastoral staffs, crucifixes, incessant bowings, turnings, and genuflections, or any such pernicious trumpery. Such things are mere gaudy toys, which may please children, and satisfy idle young men and women, and the whole herd of the ignorant, the

---

19 *A Self-Portrait*, pages 74-75.

weak-minded, and the superstitious. But they do not meet the wants of the middle-aged, the hard-headed, the hard-working men and women of the middle and lower orders. They want food—food for heart, and food for conscience; and if they do not find it in the Established Church of England, they will walk off and seek it elsewhere. Give them plain, simple, hearty Bible worship—plain, simple, hearty Bible preaching. Give them the old, old story of Christ upon the cross, the real work of the Holy Ghost felt and experienced in the inner man. Give them the noble lessons of repentance, faith, holiness. Give them these, and they will never forsake the Church of England.

After Laud we are introduced to Samuel Ward, a local hero for Ryle but a comparatively unknown figure for most people today. Ryle wrote the introduction to a reprint of Ward's works, because he too was, as he said, "thirty-seven years a Suffolk minister, and a thorough lover of Puritan theology." It is clear from the meretricious detail in this chapter that Ryle spent many happy hours researching Ward who, despite being imprisoned for nonconformity, was "so good a friend to the Church of England that he was the means of retaining several persons who were wavering about conformity, within the pale of the Episcopal communion."

We ought never to contrast Puritan and Anglican/Episcopalian, as if they were polar opposites. "That our modern conception of Anglicanism commonly excludes puritanism," said Professor Patrick Collinson, "is both a distortion of a part of our religious history and a memorial to one of its more regrettable episodes."[20] J. C. Ryle would heartily agree. As he said in 1890, "The Puritans were not enemies to the Church of England. They would gladly have seen her government and ceremonial improved, and more liberty allowed to her ministers in the conduct of public worship. But the bulk of them were originally ordained by Bishops, and had no special objection either to Episcopacy or a Liturgy."[21]

---

20 Patrick Collinson, *The Elizabethan Puritan Movement* (Oxford: Clarendon press, 1967), page 467. I have expanded this point myself in "1662 and All That" in *Truth at All Costs: Papers Read at the 2012 Westminster Conference* (Stoke-on-Trent: Tentmaker, 2013), pages 13-15.

21 *Light from Old Times* (1890), page xvi.

With an eye on that issue of staying in the Church of England despite all its faults and foibles, Ryle then turns to another Suffolk worthy, William Gurnall. Why is Gurnall not better known, he asks, since he was a leading divine, minister of a large church, and a excellent author? "He did not secede from the Church of England!" he exclaims, and that is the reason he languishes in obscurity. "Gurnall stood fast and refused to move… He was a Puritan in doctrine, and yet he steadfastly adhered to the Church of England. He was a minister of the Church of England, and yet a thorough Puritan both in preaching and practice. In fact, he was just the man to be disliked and slighted by both sides." Yet Ryle seeks to rescue him for us, because none of the great Suffolk divines he studied "appear to deserve excavation from undeserved oblivion so much as Gurnall."

It is evident, considering our own situation today, why studying the life, doctrine, and ministry of such a man might be useful. We are tested and tempted by all things silly and salacious as members of a sadly diminishing Established Church that has to a large extent sold its biblical birthright for messy liberal fudge. We are sometimes deeply disturbed by many of the compromises and official statements made by the centre, and struggle to maintain our spiritual and emotional moorings. But as Ryle says of Gurnall, who did not become a nonconformist, "while I protest against the Act of Uniformity as an unjust, unwise, impolitic, unstatesmanlike, and hard measure, I do not for a moment admit that no good man could possibly submit to its requirements." Indeed, "it is better to put up with some things we do not like in a Church, than to throw away opportunities of usefulness." Perhaps the courageously conforming puritans have as much to teach us as those who were ejected? "So long as they were allowed to preach sound doctrine, they ought not to refuse the opportunity, but to preach, and stand by their flocks."

Finally, in what was originally two *Churchman* articles from 1880, Ryle turns to the valiant endeavours of the seven bishops who resisted James II.[22] The short reign of that unhappy monarch was extremely signifi-

---

22 The biographies here were published in various ways during the nineteenth century. As

cant for the long term future of the kingdom, and yet it is less appreciated now than it ought to be. "Short as his reign was," says Ryle, "it is no exaggeration to say that it contains a more disgraceful list of cruel, stupid, unjust, and tyrannical actions, for which the Sovereign alone can be held responsible, than the reign of any constitutional monarch of this land, with the single exception of Bloody Mary." He outlines especially the way in which James sought to pull down Protestantism through the now-standard mixture of cruelty, persecution, legal censures, academic bullying, and the marginalisation of those who would not kow-tow to his policy.

After such despicable tales, we then hear about the audacious bishops who dared to stand up to the tyrannical new order. Curiously, says Ryle,

> not one of the seven men… could be called a remarkable man in any way. Not one… has made any mark in the theological world, or lives as a writer or preacher. Not one of the whole seven could be named in the same breath with Parker, or Whitgift, or Grindal, or Jewel, or Andrews, or Hall. They were probably respectable, worthy, quiet, old-fashioned High Churchmen; and that was all. But God loves to be glorified by using weak instruments.

They were imprisoned for making a stand against the will of the government, and the population respected and admired them for doing so. "Episcopacy," Ryle comments, "was never so popular as it was that week." It might recapture such popularity in future also, if it learned (like those brave brother bishops) to stiffen its neck, stand straight and true, and not buckle under state or cultural pressure.

---

mentioned above, Baxter originally appeared alongside Latimer and Whitefield in 1854. Ward, Baxter, and Gurnall were published together along with biographies of sixteenth-century bishops Hooper and Latimer in *Bishops and Clergy of Other Days* (1868). This was expanded with more sixteenth- and more seventeenth-century saints (plus John Wycliffe from the fourteenth century) in *Light from Old Times* (1890). This present volume is, I believe, the first time all of Ryle's seventeenth century material has been published together as a unique collection.

Ryle's message for today

The writer of these chapters was a keen Protestant, Evangelical churchman and pastor. In later days he was also himself a Bishop. He knew the pressures of that office, the pressures to compromise and tolerate and water-down for the sake of an easier, calmer life. "Unity and peace are very delightful," he confesses below,

> but they are bought too dear if they are bought at the expense of truth. There is a vast amount of maundering, childish, weak talk nowadays in some quarters about unity and peace, which I cannot reconcile with the language of St. Paul.

Controversy is inevitable in the church, and is the backdrop against which we are called to be faithful to Christ, in promoting and defending the truth of his word—whether we are bishops, clergy, or laity. Even if we are a small minority, it should not cause us to despair. It was ever thus.

> Yes! Evangelical clergymen are a minority in every Diocese, in every Convocation, in every Diocesan Conference, in every Congress; and they must not be surprised to find it so. But I charge them, and especially the younger men, to remember that majorities possess no more monopoly of truth and wisdom today than they did in the days of Athanasius. I beseech them, for the sake of Christ and their country, to stand firm, to stand together, never to compromise, and never to sacrifice a single vital principle under the vain pretence of obtaining unity and peace… Why should they be afraid, and faint-hearted, and weak-kneed, and give way by little and little?[23]

For Ryle it was essential that the Church of England remain true to the principled comprehensiveness defined by the *Thirty-nine Articles* and the mighty Reformation doctrines they proclaim. Whether others would step forward to defend and assert that gospel, he would not be found wanting.

May the following pages instil in all their readers that same passion

---

[23] From Ryle's introduction to *Light from Old Times*, page xxix.

and conviction, and may the Church of England never be lacking in leaders or people who are willing and able to follow the example of this great cloud of witnesses, living and suffering for Christ.

ad Dei gloriam, pro Angliae bono

Lee Gatiss
Church Society, Cambridge

A note on this edition

I have updated spelling in several places, as well as attempting to make punctuation and paragraphing more readable by modern standards. Most footnotes below are Ryle's own, except where specifically indicated. I have added biblical references where I thought it might be necessary. All headings and subheadings are mine, and I have attempted to translate Ryle's Latin where necessary.

CHRISTIAN LEADERS
OF THE SEVENTEENTH CENTURY

BY *J.C. Ryle*

1. Richard Baxter

There are subjects about which it is well to look behind us. There are matters in which a knowledge of the past may teach us wisdom for the present and the future. The history of religion is pre-eminently such a subject and matter. Steam, electricity, railways, and gas, have made a wonderful difference in the temporal condition of mankind in the last two hundred years. But all this time the Bible and the hearts of men have remained unaltered. That which men did and thought in religious matters two hundred years ago, they are capable of doing and thinking again.

What they thought and did in England in the seventeenth century it is well to know. And just as there are subjects about which it is wise to look behind us, so also there are times long gone by which deserve our special attention. There are times when the character of a nation receives an indelible impression from events which take place in a single generation. There have been times when the dearest privileges of a people have been brought to the birth, and called into vigorous existence, through the desperate agony of civil war and religious strife. Such, I take leave to say, were the times of which I am about to speak in this biography.

To no times are Englishmen so deeply indebted for their civil and religious liberty as the times in which Baxter lived. To no body of men do they owe such an unpaid debt of gratitude as they do to that noble host of which Baxter was a standard bearer: I mean the Puritans. To no man among the Puritans are the lovers of religious freedom under such large obligations as they are to Richard Baxter.

I am fully sensible of the difficulties which surround the subject. It is a subject which few historians handle fairly, simply because they do not understand spiritual religion. To an unconverted man the religious differences of the day of the Puritans must necessarily appear foolishness. He is no more qualified to give an opinion about them than a blind man is to talk of pictures. It is a subject which no clergyman of the Church of England can approach without laying himself open to misrepresentation. He will be suspected of disaffection to his own Church if he speaks favourably of men who opposed Bishops. But it is a subject on which it is most important for Englishmen to have distinct opinions, and I must ask for it a patient hearing. If I can correct some false impressions, if I can supply a few great principles to guide men in these perilous times, I feel I shall have done my readers an essential service. And if I fail to interest them in "Baxter and his Times," I am sure the fault is not in the subject, but in me.

The times in which Baxter lived comprehend such a vast amount of interesting matter, that I must of necessity leave many points in their history entirely untouched.

My meaning will be plain when I say that he was born in 1615, and died in 1691. Nearly all his life was passed under the dynasty of a house which reigned over England with no benefit to the country and no credit to itself: I mean the Stuarts. He lived through the reign of James I, Charles I, Charles II, and James II, and was buried in the reign of William III. He was in the prime of life and intellectual vigour all through the days of the Commonwealth and the civil wars. He witnessed the overthrow of the Monarchy and the Church of England, and their subsequent re-establishment. He was a contemporary of Cromwell, of Laud, of Strafford, of Hampden, of Pym, of Monck, of Clarendon, of Milton, of Hale, of Jeffreys, of Blake.

In his days took place the public execution of an English Monarch,

Charles I; of an Archbishop of Canterbury, Laud; and of a Lord Lieutenant of Ireland, Strafford. Within the single period of his life are to be found the plague, the fire of London, the Westminster Assembly, the Long Parliament, the Savoy Conference, and the rejection of two thousand of the best ministers of the Church of England by the Act of Uniformity.

Remarkable Features of the Seventeenth Century

Such were the eventful times in which Baxter lived. I cannot, of course, pretend to enter fully into them. Their history forms a huge picture, like the moving panorama of the Mississippi, which it is utterly impossible to take in at a glance. I shall simply try to fix attention on a few of the leading features of the picture, and I shall choose those points which appear to me most likely to be useful in the present day.

Moving away from Protestantism

One remarkable feature in the history of Baxter's times is the move backward from the principles of the Protestant Reformation, which commenced in his youth. Doctrines and practices began to be maintained, both by preachers and writers in the Church of England, which Latimer and Jewell would never have sanctioned. Sound Evangelical teaching was decried and run down, under the specious name of 'Calvinism.' Good bishops, like Davenant, were snubbed and reprimanded. Bad bishops, like Montague and Wren, were patted on the back and encouraged. Preaching and lecturing were depreciated, and forms and ceremonies were exalted. The benefits of Episcopacy were extravagantly magnified.

Candlesticks and crosses, and all manner of Popish ornaments, were introduced into some of the churches. The sanctity of the Lord's Day was invaded by the abominable Book of Sports, and common people were encouraged to spend Sunday in England as it is now spent in France. The communion tables, which up to this time had stood in the middle of the chancel, were removed to the east end of the churches, put behind rails, and profanely called "altars." Against all these sapping and mining operations some, no doubt, protested loudly; but still the sappers and miners went on.

The prime agent in the whole movement was Archbishop Laud. Whether that unhappy man really intended to re-unite the Church of England with the Church of Rome is a question which will probably never be settled till the last day. One thing is very certain —no one could have played the game of Rome more thoroughly than he did.

Like many a mischief-maker before and since, Laud pulled the house in which he lived upon his own head. He raised a storm at length, before which the Church, the Throne, and the bishops, all went down together, and in the midst of which he himself was put on his trial and lost his life. But the Church of England received an injury in Laud's days from which it has never entirely recovered. Since his time there never has been wanting a succession of men amongst its ministers who have held most of Laud's principles, and occasionally have boldly walked in his steps. So true are the words of Shakespeare, "The evil that men do lives after them."

The harm that Queen Mary did to the Church of England was nothing compared to the harm done by Laud. We must never underrate the mischief that one bold, bad man can do, and especially in matters of religion. The seeds of error are like thistle-down. One head of a thistle scattered by the wind will sow a whole field. One Tom Paine can rear up infidels all over the world. One Laud can leaven generations with untold mischief. Never let us suppose that extreme Ritualism is a legitimate child of the Church of England. It is not so. It was scarcely heard of till the time of the Stuarts. Never let us suppose that Tractarianism, or Ritualism, so called, is a new invention of these latter days. It is not so. It is two hundred years old. The father of extreme Ritualists is Archbishop Laud. Let us remember these things, and we shall have learned something from Baxter's times.

The Civil Wars

Another remarkable feature in the history of Baxter's times is the famous civil war between Charles I and his Parliament.

All war is an evil—a necessary evil sometimes—but still an evil; and of all wars, the most distressing is a civil war. It is a kind of huge family quarrel. It is a struggle in which victory brings no glory, because the strife has been the strife of brethren. Edge Hill, and Newbury, and Marston Moor, and Naseby, and Worcester, are names which call up none but painful reflections. The victors in each battle had spilt the blood of their own countrymen, and lessened the general strength of the nation.

But there is a point of view in which the civil war between Charles I and his Parliament was peculiarly distressing. I allude to the striking fact, that the general irreligion and immorality of the King's party did more to ruin his cause than all the armies which the Parliament raised. There were hundreds and thousands of steady, quiet men, who, at the beginning of the war, were desirous to be still, and help neither side. But when they found that a man could not read his Bible to his dependents and have prayer in his family without being persecuted as a Roundhead, they felt obliged, in self-defence, to join the Parliamentary forces.

In plain words, the wickedness and profligacy of many of the Cavaliers drove godly men into the ranks of their enemies. That there was plenty of hypocrisy, fanaticism, and enthusiasm on the Parliamentary side, I make no question. That there were some good men among the Cavaliers, such as Lord Falkland, I do not deny. But, after every allowance, I have no doubt there was far more true religion among those who fought for the Parliament than among those who fought for the King.

The result of the civil war, under these peculiar circumstances, never need surprise any one who knows human nature. The drinking, swearing, roistering troopers, who were led by Prince Rupert, and Wilmot, and Goring, proved no match for the praying, psalm-singing, Bible-reading men whom Cromwell, and Fairfax, and Ireton, and Harrison, and Fleetwood, and Desborough, brought into the field. The steadiest men will in the long run make the best soldiers. A side which has a strong religious principle among its supporters will seldom be a losing one. "Those who honour God, God will honour; and they that despise Him shall be lightly esteemed" (1 Samuel 2:30).

I shall dismiss the subject of the civil war with one general remark and one caution.

My general remark is that, deeply as we must regret the civil war, we must in fairness remember that we probably owe to it the free and excellent Constitution which we possess in this country. God can bring good out of evil. The oscillations of England between despotism and anarchy, and anarchy and despotism, for many years after the breach between Charles I and the House of Commons, were certainly tremendously violent. Still we must confess, that great political lessons were probably imprinted on the English mind at that period, of which we are reaping the benefit at this very day. Monarchs were taught that, like planets in heaven, they must be content to move in a certain orbit, and that an enlightened people would not be governed and taxed without the consent of an unfettered House of Commons. Nations were taught that it is a far easier thing to pull to pieces than to build, and to upset an ancient monarchy than to find a government which shall be a satisfactory substitute. Many of the foundations of our choicest national privileges, I make no doubt, were laid in the Commonwealth times. We shall do well to remember this. We may rest satisfied that this country owes an immense debt of gratitude to Brooke, and Hampden, and Eliot, and Whitelock, and Pym.

The caution I wish to give respects the execution of Charles I. We shall do well to remember that the great bulk of the Puritans were entirely guiltless of any participation in the trial and death of the King. It is a vulgar error to suppose, as many do, that the whole Parliamentary party are accountable for that wicked and impolitic act. The immense majority of the Presbyterians protested loudly against it. Baxter tells us expressly in his autobiography, that together with many other ministers he declared his abhorrence of it, and used every exertion to prevent it. The deed was the doing of Cromwell and his immediate adherents in the army, and it is at their door that the whole guilt must lie. That the great body of the Puritans espoused the Parliamentary side there is no doubt. But as to any abstract dislike to royalty, or assent to King Charles's death, the Puritans are entirely innocent. Let us remember this, and we shall have learned something from the history of Baxter's times.

The Rise of Oliver Cromwell

The next feature in the history of Baxter's times, to which I shall venture to call attention, is the rise and conduct of that remarkable man, Oliver Cromwell.

There are few men on whose character more obloquy has been heaped than Oliver Cromwell. He has been painted by some as a monster of wickedness and hypocrisy. Nothing has been too bad to say of him. Such an estimate of him is simply ridiculous. It defeats the end of those who form it. They forget that it is no compliment to England to suppose that it would so long tolerate the rule of such a monster. The man who could raise himself from being the son of a brewer at Huntingdon to be the most successful general of his age, and absolute dictator of this country for many years, must, on the very face of facts, have been a most extraordinary man.

For my own part I say frankly, that I think we ought to consider the estimate of Cromwell, which Carlyle and D'Aubigné have formed, to be a near approach to the truth. I own I cannot go the lengths of the latter writer. I dare not pronounce positively that Cromwell was a sincere Christian. I leave the question in suspense. I hazard no opinion about it, one way or the other, because I do not find sufficient materials for forming an opinion. If I were to look at his private letters only, I should not hesitate to call him a converted man. But when I look at some of his public acts, I see much that appears to me quite inexplicable. And when I observe how doubtfully Baxter and other good men, who were his contemporaries, speak of him, my hesitancy as to his spirituality is much increased. In short, I turn from the question in a state of doubt.

That Oliver Cromwell was one of the greatest Englishmen that ever lived I feel no doubt at all. No man, perhaps, ever won supreme power by the sword, and then used that power with such moderation as he did. England was probably more feared and respected throughout Europe, during the short time that he was Protector, than she ever was before, or ever has been since. His very name carried terror with it. He declared that he would make the name of an Englishman as great as ever that of a Roman had been. And he certainly succeeded.

He made it publicly known that he would not allow the Protestant faith to be insulted in any part of the world. And he kept his word. When the Duke of Savoy began to persecute the Vaudois in his days, Cromwell interfered at once on their behalf, and never rested till the Duke's army was recalled from their villages, and the poor people's goods and houses restored. When certain Protestants at Nismes, in France, were threatened with oppressive usage by the French government, Cromwell instructed his ambassador at Paris to insist peremptorily, that proceedings against them should be dropped, and in the event of a refusal, to leave Paris immediately. In fact, it was said that Cardinal Mazarin, the French Minister, would change countenance when Cromwell's name was mentioned; and that it was almost proverbial in France, that the Cardinal was more afraid of Cromwell than of the devil. As for the Pope, he was so dreadfully frightened by a fleet which Cromwell sent into the Mediterranean, under Blake, to settle some matters with the Duke of Tuscany, that he commanded processions to be made in Rome, and the Host to be exposed for forty hours, in order to avert the judgments of God, and save the Church. In short, the influence of English Protestantism was never so powerfully felt throughout Europe as it was in the days of Oliver Cromwell.

I will only ask my readers to remember, in addition to these facts, that Cromwell's government was remarkable for its toleration, and this, too, in an age when toleration was very little understood; that his private life was irreproachable; and that he enforced a standard of morality throughout the kingdom which was, unhappily, unknown in the days of the Stuarts. Let us remember all these things, and then I think we shall not lightly give way to the common opinion that Cromwell was a wicked and hypocritical man. Let us rest assured that his character deserves far better treatment than it has generally received hitherto. Let us regard him as one who, with all his faults, did great things for our country. Let not those faults blind our eyes to the real greatness of his character. Let us give him a high place in the list of great men before our mind's eye. Let us do this, and we shall have learned something from Baxter's times.

The Suicidal Blindness of the Church of England

There is one more feature in the history of Baxter's times which I feel it impossible to pass over. I allude to the suicidal blindness of the Church of England under the Stuarts.

I touch on this subject with some reluctance. I love the Church of which I am a minister, heartily and sincerely. But I have never found out that my Church lays claim to infallibility, and I am bound to confess that in the times of the Stuarts she committed some tremendous mistakes.

Far be it from me to say that these mistakes were chargeable upon all her members. Abbot, and Carlton, and Davenant, and Hall, and Prideaux, and Usher, and Reynolds, and Wilkins, were bright exceptions among the bishops, both as to doctrine and practice. But, unhappily, these good men were always in a minority in the Church; and the manner in which the majority administered the affairs of the Church is the subject to which I wish to call attention. We ought to know something about the subject, because it serves to throw immense light on the history of our unhappy religious divisions in this country. We ought to know something of it, because it is one which is intimately bound up with Baxter's life.

One part of the suicidal blindness of the Church to which I have referred, was its long-continued attempt to compel conformity, and prohibit private religious exercises, by pains and penalties. A regular crusade was kept up against everybody who infringed its canons, or did anything contrary to its rubrics. Hundreds and thousands of men, for many years, were summoned before magistrates, fined, imprisoned, and often ruined; not because they had offended against the gospel or the Ten Commandments, not because they had made an open attack on the Churches; but merely because they had transgressed some petty ecclesiastical by-law, more honoured in the breach than in the observance; or because they tried by quiet, private meetings to obtain some spiritual edification over and above that which the public services of the Church provided.

At one time we read of good men having their ears cut off and their noses slit, for writing unfavourably of bishops! This was the fate of the father of Archbishop Leighton! At another time we read of an enactment by which any one present at a meeting of five or more persons, where there was any exercise of religion in other manner than that allowed by the Liturgy of the Church of England, was to be fined, or imprisoned for three months for the first offence, six months for the second offence, and for the third, transported for seven years! Many were afraid to have family prayer if more than four acquaintances were present! Some families had scruples about saying grace if five strangers were at table! Such was the state of England in the seventeenth century under the Stuarts.

The result of this miserable policy was just exactly what might have been expected. There arose a spirit of deep discontent on the part of the persecuted. There sprung up among them a feeling of disaffection to the Church in which they had been baptized, and a rooted conviction that a system must necessarily be bad in principle which could bear such fruits. Men became sick of the very name of the Liturgy, when it was bound up in their memories with a fine or a gaol. Men became weary of episcopacy, when they found that bishops were more frequently a terror to good works than to evil ones. The words of Baxter, in a striking passage on this subject in his autobiography, are very remarkable: "The more the bishops thought to cure schism by punishment, the more they increased the opinion that they were persecuting enemies of godliness, and the captains of the profane."

And who that knows human nature can wonder at such a state of feeling? The mass of men will generally judge an institution by its administration, more than by its abstract excellencies. When plain Englishmen saw that a man might do almost anything so long as he did not break an ecclesiastical canon; when they saw that people might gamble, and swear, and get drunk, and no one made them afraid, but that people who met after service to sing psalms and join in prayer were heavily punished; when they saw that godless, ignorant reprobate, profligate spendthrifts, sat under their own vines and fig-trees in peace, so long as they conformed and went to their parish churches, but that humble, holy, conscientious, Bible-reading persons, who sometimes went out of their parishes to church, were severely fined; when they found that Charles the Second and his boon companions were free to waste a nation's substance in riotous living, while the saints of the nation, like Baxter and Jenkyn, were rotting in gaols—I say, when plain Englishmen saw these things, they found it hard to love the Church which did them.

Yet all this might often have been seen in many counties of England under the Stuarts. If this was not suicidal blindness on the part of the Church of England, I know not what is. It was helping the devil, by driving good men out of her communion. It was literally bleeding herself to death.

The crowning piece of folly which the majority in the Church of England committed under the Stuarts, was procuring the Act of Uniformity to be enacted in the year 1662. This, you must remember, took place at the beginning of Charles the Second's reign, and shortly after the re-establishment of the Monarchy and the Church.

This famous act imposed terms and conditions of holding office on all ministers of the Church of England which had never been imposed before, from the time of the Reformation. It was notoriously so framed as to be offensive to the consciences of the Puritans, and to drive them out of the Church. For this purpose it was entirely successful. Within a year no less than 2,000 clergymen resigned their livings rather than accept its terms. Many of these 2,000 were the best, the ablest, and the holiest ministers of the day. Many a man, who had been regularly ordained by bishops, and spent twenty or thirty years in the service of the Church without molestation, was suddenly commanded to accept new conditions of holding preferment, and turned out to starve because he refused. Sixty of the leading parishes in London were at once deprived of their ministers, and their congregations left like sheep without a shepherd. Taking all things into consideration, a more impolitic and disgraceful deed never disfigured the annals of a Protestant Church.

It was a disgraceful deed, because it was a flat contradiction to Charles the Second's own promise at Breda, before he came back from exile. He was brought back on the distinct understanding that the Church of England should be re-established on such a broad and liberal basis as to satisfy the conscientious scruples of the Puritans. Had it not been for the assistance of the Puritans he would never have got back at all. And yet as soon as the reins of power were fairly in the King's hands his promise was deliberately broken!

It was a disgraceful deed, because the great majority of the ejected ministers might easily have been retained in the Church by a few small concessions. They had no abstract objection to episcopacy, or to a liturgy. A few alterations in the prayers, and a moderate liberty in the conduct of Divine worship, according to Baxter's calculation, would have satisfied 1,600 out of the 2,000. But the ruling party were determined not to make a single concession. They had no wish to keep the Puritans in the Church. When some one observed to Archbishop Sheldon, the chief mover in the business, that he thought many of the Puritans would conform, and accept the Act of Uniformity, the Archbishop replied, "I am afraid they will." To show the spirit of the ruling party in the Church, they actually added to the number of apocryphal lessons in the Prayer Book calendar at this time. They made it a matter of congratulation among themselves that they had thrust out the Puritans, and got in *Bel and the Dragon!*

It was a disgraceful deed, because the ejected ministers were, many of them, men of such ability and attainments, that great concessions ought to have been made in order to retain them in the Church. Baxter, Poole, Manton, Bates, Calamy, Brooks, Watson, Charnock, Caryl, Howe, Flavel, Bridge, Jenkyn, Owen, Goodwin, are names whose praise is even now in all the Churches. The men who turned them out were not to be compared to them. The names of the vast majority of them are hardly known. But they had power on their side, and they were resolved to use it.

It was a disgraceful deed, because it showed the world that the leaders of the Church of England, like the Bourbons in modern times, had learned nothing and forgotten nothing during their exile. They had not forgotten the old bad ways of Laud, which had brought such misery on England. They had not learned that conciliation and concession are the most becoming graces in the rulers of a Church, and that persecution in the long run is sure to be a losing game.

I dare not dwell longer on this point. I might easily bring forward more illustrations of this sad feature in Baxter's times. I might speak of the infamous Oxford Act, in 1665, which forbade the unhappy ejected ministers to live within five miles of any corporate town, or of any place where they had formerly preached. But enough has been said to show that when I spoke of the suicidal blindness of the Church of England, I did not speak without cause. The consequences of this blindness are manifest to any one who knows England. The divided state of Protestantism in this country is of itself a great fact, which speaks volumes.

Against the policy of the ruling party in the Church of England, under the Stuarts, I always shall protest. I do not feel the scruples which Baxter and his ejected brethren felt about the Act of Uniformity. Much as I respect them, I think them wrong and misguided in their judgments. But I think that Archbishop Sheldon, and the men who refused to go one step to meet them, were far more wrong and far more misguided. I believe they did an injury to the cause of true religion in England, which will probably never be repaired, by sowing the seeds of endless divisions. They were the men who laid the foundation of English dissent. I believe they recklessly threw away a golden opportunity of doing good. They might easily have made my own beloved Church far more effective and far more useful than she ever has been by wise and timely concessions. They refused to do this, and, instead of a healing measure, brought forward their unhappy Act of Uniformity. I disavow any sympathy with their proceedings, and can never think of them without the deepest regret.

I cannot leave the subject of Baxter's times without offering one piece of counsel to my readers. I advise you, then, not to believe everything you may happen to read on the subject of the times of the Stuarts. There are no times, perhaps, about which prejudice and party-spirit have so warped the judgment and jaundiced the eye-sight of historians. If any one wants a really fair and impartial history of the times, I strongly advise him to read Marsden's *History of the Puritans*. I regard these two volumes as the most valuable addition which has been made to our stock of religious history in modern times.

The Life of Richard Baxter

I now turn from Baxter's times to Baxter himself. Without some knowledge of the times, we can hardly understand the character and conduct of the man. A few plain facts about the man will be more likely than anything I can write to fasten in our minds the times.

Richard Baxter was the son of a small landed proprietor of Eaton Constantine in Shropshire, and was born, in 1615 at Rowton, in the same county, where Mr. Adeney, his mother's father, resided.

He seems to have been under religious impressions from a very early period of his life, and for this, under God, he was indebted to the training of a pious father. Shropshire was a very dark, ungodly county in those days. The ministers were generally ignorant, graceless, and unable to preach; and the people, as might be expected, were profligate, and despisers of them that were good. In Eaton Constantine, the parishioners spent the greater part of the Lord's Day in dancing round a Maypole near old Mr. Baxter's door, to his great distress and annoyance. Yet even here grace triumphed over the world in the case of his son, and he was added to the noble host of those who "serve the Lord from their youth."

It is always interesting to observe the names of religious books, which God is pleased to use in bringing souls to the knowledge of himself. The books which had the most effect on Baxter were Bunny's *Resolution*; Perkins *On Repentance, On Living and Dying Well*, and *On the Government of the Tongue*; Culverwell *On Faith*; and Sibbe's *Bruised Reed*. Disease and the prospect of death did much to carry on the spiritual work within him. He says in his autobiography, "Weakness and pain helped me to study how to die. That set me on studying how to live, and that on studying the doctrines from which I must fetch my motives and my comforts."

At the age of twenty-two he was ordained a clergyman, by Thornborough, Bishop of Worcester. He had never had the advantage of a University education. A free school at Wroxeter, and a private tutor at Ludlow, had done something for him; and his own insatiable love of study had done a good deal more. He, probably, entered the ministry far better furnished with theological learning than most young men of his day. He certainly entered it with qualifications far better than a knowledge of Greek and Hebrew. He entered it truly moved by the Holy Ghost, and a converted man. He says himself, "I knew that the want of academical honours and degrees were like to make me contemptible with the most. But yet, expecting to be so quickly in another world, the great concernment of miserable souls did prevail with me against all impediments. And being conscious of a thirsty desire of men's conscience and salvation, I resolved, that if one or two souls only might be won to God, it would easily recompense all the dishonour which, for want of titles, I might undergo from men."

From the time of his ordination to his death, Baxter's life was a constant series of strange vicissitudes, and intense physical and mental exertions. Sometimes in prosperity and sometimes in adversity, sometimes praised and sometimes persecuted. At one period catechising in the lanes of Kidderminster; at another disputing with bishops in the Savoy Conference. One year writing the "Saint's Rest," at the point of death, in a quiet country house; another year a marching chaplain to a regiment in Cromwell's army. One day offered a bishopric by Charles II; another cast out of the Church by the Act of Uniformity. One year arguing for monarchy with Cromwell, and telling him it was a blessing; another tried before Jeffreys on a charge of seditious writing. One time living quietly at Acton in the society of Judge Hale; at another languishing in prison under some atrocious ecclesiastical persecution. One day having public discussions about infant baptism, with Mr. Tombes in Bewdley Church; another holding the reading-desk of Amersham Church from morning to night against the theological arguments of Antinomian dragoons in the gallery. Sometimes preaching the plainest doctrines; sometimes handling the most abstruse metaphysical points. Sometimes writing folios for the learned; sometimes writing broad-sheets for the poor.

Never, perhaps, did any Christian minister fill so many various positions; and never, certainly, did any one come out of them all with such an unblemished reputation. Always suffering under incurable disease, and seldom long out of pain. Always working his mind to the uttermost, and never idle for a day. Seemingly overwhelmed with business, and yet never refusing new work. Living in the midst of the most exciting scenes, and yet holding daily converse with God. Not sufficiently a partisan to satisfy any side, and yet feared and courted by all. Too much of a Royalist to please the Parliamentary party, and yet too much connected with the Parliament and too holy to be popular with the Cavaliers. Too much of an Episcopalian to satisfy the violent portion of the Puritan body, and too much of a Puritan to be trusted by the bishops. Never, probably, did Christian man enjoy so little rest, though serving God with a pure conscience, as did Richard Baxter.

In 1638 he began his ministry, by preaching in the Upper Church at Dudley. There he continued a year. From Dudley he removed to

Bridgnorth. There he continued a year and three-quarters. From Bridgnorth he removed to Kidderminster. From thence, after two years, he retired to Coventry, at the beginning of the Commonwealth troubles, and awaited the progress of the civil war. From Coventry, after the battle of Naseby, he joined the Parliamentary army in the capacity of Regimental Chaplain. He took this office in the vain hope that he might do some good among the soldiers, and counteract the ambitious designs of Cromwell and his friends. He was obliged by illness to give up his chaplaincy in 1646, and lingered for some months between life and death at the hospitable houses of Sir John Coke of Melbourne in Derbyshire, and Sir Thomas Rous of Rouslench in Worcestershire. At the end of 1646 he returned to Kidderminster, and there continued labouring indefatigably as parish Minister for fourteen years.

In 1660 he left Kidderminster for London, and took an active part in promoting the restoration of Charles II, and was made one of the King's Chaplains. In London, he preached successively at St. Dunstan's, Black Friars', and St. Bride's. Shortly after this he was offered the Bishopric of Hereford, but thought fit to refuse it. In 1662 he was one of the 2000 ministers who were turned out of the Church by the Act of Uniformity.

Immediately after his ejection he married a wife who seems to have been every way worthy of him, and who was spared to be his loving and faithful companion for nineteen years. Her name was Margaret Charlton, of Apley Castle in Shropshire. After this he lived in various places in and about London—at Acton, Totteridge, Bloomsbury, and at last in Charterhouse Square. The disgraceful treatment of his enemies made it almost impossible for him to have any certain dwelling place. Once, at this period of his life, he was offered a Scotch Bishopric, or the Mastership of a Scotch University, but declined both offices. With few exceptions, the last twenty-nine years of his life were embittered by repeated prosecutions, fines, imprisonment, and harassing controversies. When he could he preached, and when he could not preach he wrote books; but something he was always doing. The revolution and accession of William III brought him some little respite from persecution, and death at last removed the good old man to that place "where the wicked cease from troubling and the weary are at rest," in the year 1691, and the seventy-sixth year of his age.

Baxter's Qualities

Such is a brief outline of the life of one of the most distinguished Puritans who lived under the Stuarts, and one of the most devoted ministers of the gospel this country has ever seen. It is an outline which, we may readily believe, might be filled up to an indefinite length. I cannot, of course, pretend to do more than direct attention to a few leading particulars. If I do not tell more, it is not from want of matter. But if any one wishes to know why Baxter's name stands so high as it does in the list of English worthies, I ask him to give me his attention for a few minutes, and I will soon show him cause.

For one thing, Baxter was a man of most eminent personal holiness. Few men have ever lived before the eyes of the world for fifty or sixty years, as he did, and left so fair and unblemished a reputation. Bitterly and cruelly as many hated him, they could find no fault in the man, except "concerning the law of his God." He seems to have been holy in all the relations of life, and in all the circumstances in which man can be placed: holy as a son, a husband, a minister, and a friend; holy in prosperity and in adversity, in sickness and in health, in youth and in old age. It is a fine saying of Orme, in his admirable life of him, that he was, in the highest sense, a most "unearthly" man. He lived with God, and Christ, and heaven, and death, and judgment, and eternity continually before his eyes. He cared nothing for the good things of this world: a bishopric, with all its emoluments and honours, had no charms for him. He cared nothing for the enmity of the world: no fear of man's displeasure ever turned him an inch out of his way. He was singularly independent of man's praise or blame. He could be bold as a lion in the presence of Cromwell or Charles II, and his bishops; and yet he could be gentle as a lamb with poor people seeking how to be saved. He could be zealous as a Crusader for the rights of conscience, and yet he was of so catholic a spirit that he loved all who loved Jesus Christ in sincerity.

"Be it by Conformists or by Nonconformists," he would say, "I rejoice that Christ is preached." He was a truly humble man. To one who wrote to him expressing admiration for his character, he replied, "You admire one you do not know: knowledge would cure your error." So fair an epistle of Christ, considering the amazing trials of patience he had to go through, this country has seldom seen as Richard Baxter. Let us remember this point in Baxter's character. No argument has such lasting power with the world as a holy and consistent life. Let us remember that this holiness was attained by a man of like passions with ourselves. Let Baxter be an encouragement and an example. Let us remember the Lord God of Baxter is not changed.

For another thing, Baxter was one of the most powerful preachers that ever addressed an English congregation. He seems to have possessed all the gifts which are generally considered to make a perfect "master of assemblies." He had an amazing fluency, an enormous store of matter, a most clear and lucid style, an unlimited command of forcible language, a pithy, pointed, emphatic way of presenting truth, a singularly moving and pathetic voice, and an earnestness of manner which swept everything before it like a torrent. He used to say, "It must be serious preaching which will make men serious in hearing and obeying it." Two well-known lines of his show you the man: "I'll preach as though I ne'er should preach again, And as a dying man to dying men."

Dr. Bates, a contemporary, says of him, "He had a marvellous felicity and copiousness in speaking. There was a noble negligence in his style. His great mind could not stoop to the affected eloquence of words. He despised flashy oratory. But his expressions were so clear and powerful, so convincing to the understanding, so entering into the soul, so engaging the affections, that those were as deaf as an adder who were not charmed by so wise a charmer."

The effects that his preaching produced were those which such preaching always has produced, and always will. As it was under the pulpit of

Latimer and Whitefield, so it was under the pulpit of Baxter. At Dudley the poor nailers would not only crowd the church, but even hang upon the windows and the leads without. At Kidderminster it became necessary to build five new galleries, in order to accommodate the congregation. In London the crowds who attended his ministry were so large that it was sometimes dangerous, and often impossible, to be one of his hearers.

Once, when he was about to preach at St. Lawrence, Jewry, he sent word to Mr. Vines, the minister, that the Earl of Suffolk and Lord Broghill were coming in a coach with him, and would be glad to have seats. But when he and his noble companions reached the door, the crowd had so little respect for persons, that the two peers had to go home again because they could not get within hearing. Mr. Vines himself was obliged to get up into the pulpit, and sit behind the preacher, from want of room; and Baxter actually preached standing between Mr. Vine's feet.

On another occasion, when he was preaching to an enormous crowd in St. Dunstan's, Fleet Street he made a striking use of an incident which took place during the sermon. A piece of brick fell down in the steeple, and an alarm was raised that the church, an old and rotten building, was falling. Scarcely was the alarm allayed, when a bench, on which some people were standing, broke with their weight, and the confusion was worse than ever. Many crowded to the doors to get out, and all were in a state of panic. One old woman was heard loudly asking God forgiveness for having come to the church at all, and promising, if she only got out safe, never to come there again. In the midst of all the confusion Baxter alone was calm and unmoved. As soon as order was restored, he rose and said, "We are in the service of God to prepare ourselves that we may be fearless at the great noise of the dissolving world, when the heavens shall pass away, and the elements melt with fervent heat."

This was Baxter all over. This was the kind of thing he had not only grace, but gifts and nerve, to do. He always spoke like one who saw God, and felt death at his back. Such a man will seldom fail to preach well.

Such a man will seldom be in want of hearers. Such a man deserves to be embalmed in the memory of all who want to know what God can do for a child of Adam by his Spirit. Such a man deserves to be praised.

For another thing, Baxter was one of the most successful pastors of a parish and congregation that ever lived. When he came to Kidderminster he found it a dark, ignorant, immoral, irreligious place, containing, perhaps, 3,000 inhabitants. When he left it, at the end of fourteen years, he had completely turned the parish upside down. "The place before his coming," says Dr. Bates, "was like a piece of dry and barren earth; but, by the blessing of heaven upon his labour, the face of Paradise appeared there. The bad were changed to good, and the good to better." The number of his regular communicants averaged 600. "Of these," Baxter tells us, "there were not twelve of whom I had not good hope as to their sincerity." The Lord's Day was thoroughly reverenced and observed. It was said, "You might have heard an hundred families singing psalms and repeating sermons as you passed through the streets."

When he came there, there was about one family in a street which worshipped God at home. When he went away, there were some streets in which there was not more than one family on a side that did not do it; and this was the case even with inns and public houses. Even of the irreligious families, there were very few which had not some converted relations. "Some of the poor people became so well versed in theology that they understood the whole body of divinity, and were able to judge difficult controversies. Some were so able in prayer that few ministers could match them in order, fulness, apt expressions, holy oratory, and fervour. Best of all, the temper of their minds and the innocency of their lives were much more laudable even than their gifts."

The grand instrument to which Baxter used to attribute this astounding success, was his system of household visitation and regular private conference with his parishioners. No doubt this did immense good, and the more so because it was a new thing in those days. Nevertheless, there is no denying the fact that the most elaborate parochial machinery of modern times has never produced such effects as those you have just heard of at Kidderminster. And the true account of this I believe to be, that no parish has ever had such a wonderful mainspring in the middle of it as Baxter was. While some divines were wrangling about the divine right of Episcopacy or Presbytery, or splitting hairs about reprobation and free-will, Baxter was always visiting from house to house, and beseeching men, for Christ's sake, to be reconciled to God and flee from the wrath to come. While others were entangling themselves in politics, and "burying their dead" amidst the potsherds of the earth, Baxter was living a crucified life, and daily preaching the gospel. I suspect he was the best and wisest pastor that an English parish has ever had, and a model that many a modern rector or vicar would do well to follow. Once more I say, have I not a right to say such a polished instrument as this ought not to be allowed to rust in oblivion? Such a man as this deserves to be praised.

For another thing, Baxter was one of the most diligent theological writers the world has ever seen. Few have the slightest idea of the immense number of works in divinity which he wrote in the fifty years of his active life. It is reckoned that they would fill sixty octavo volumes, comprising not less than 35,000 closely-printed pages. These works, no doubt, are not all of equal merit, and many of them probably will never repay perusal. Like the ships from Tarshish, they contain not only gold, and silver, and ivory, but also a large quantity of apes and peacocks (1 Kings 10:22).

Still, after every deduction, the writings of Baxter generally contain a great mass of solid truths, and truths often handled in a most striking and masterly way. Dr. Barrow, no mean judge, says "That his practical writings were never mended, and his controversial ones seldom confuted." Bishop Wilkins declares "That he had cultivated every subject he had handled, that if he had lived in the primitive times he would have been one of the Fathers of the Church, and that it was enough for one age to produce such a man as Mr. Baxter." That great and good man, William Wilberforce, says, "His practical writings are a treasury of Christian wisdom"; and he adds, "I must beg to class among the brightest ornaments of the Church of England this great man, who was so shamefully ejected from the Church in 1662."

No one man has certainly ever written three such books as Baxter's three masterpieces, *The Saint's Rest*, *The Reformed Pastor*, and *The Call to the Unconverted*. I believe they have been made blessings to thousands of souls, and are alone sufficient to place the author in the foremost rank of theological writers. Of *The Call to the Unconverted*, 20,000 were printed in one year. Six brothers were converted at one time by reading it. Eliot, the missionary, thought so highly of it that he translated it into the Indian language, the first book after the Bible. And really, when we consider that all Baxter's writings were composed in the midst of intense labour and fierce persecution, and often under the pressure of heavy bodily disease, the wonder is not only that he wrote so much, but that so much of what he wrote should be so good. Such wonderful diligence and redemption of time the world has never seen. Once more I say, have I not a right to say such a man deserves to be praised?

For another thing, Baxter was one of the most patient martyrs for conscience's sake that England has ever seen. Of course I do not mean that he was called upon to seal his faith with his blood, as our Protestant Reformers were. But there is such a thing as "wearing out the saints of the Most High" (Daniel 7:25) by persecutions and prisons, as well as shedding the blood of the saints. There is a "dying daily," which, to some natures, is worse even than dying at the stake. If anything tries faith and patience I believe it to be the constant dropping of such wearing persecution as Baxter had to endure for nearly the last twenty-nine years of his life. He had robbed no one. He had murdered no one. He had injured no one. He held no heresy. He believed all the Articles of the Christian faith. And yet no thief or felon in the present day was ever so shamefully treated as this good man. To tell you how often he was summoned, fined, silenced, imprisoned, driven from one place to another, would be an endless task. To describe all the hideous perversions of justice to which he was subjected would be both painful and unprofitable. I will only allow myself to give one instance, and that shall be his trial before Chief Justice

Jeffreys.

Baxter was tried before Jeffreys in 1685, at Westminster Hall, on a charge of having published seditious matter, reflecting on the bishops, in a paraphrase on the New Testament which he had recently brought out. A more unfounded charge could not have been made. The book is still extant, and any one will see at a glance that the alleged seditious passages do not prove the case. Fox, in his history of James II's reign, tells us plainly "that the real motive for bringing him to trial was the desire of punishing an eminent dissenting teacher, whose reputation was high among his sect, and who was supposed to favour the political opinions of the Whigs."

A long and graphic account of the trial was drawn up by a bystander, and it gives so vivid a picture of the administration of justice in Baxter's days that it may be useful to give a few short extracts from it.

From the very opening of the trial it was clear which way the verdict was intended to go. The Lord Chief Justice of England behaved as if he were counsel for the prosecution, and not judge. He condescended to use abusive language towards the defendant, such as was more suited to Billingsgate than a court of law. One after another the counsel for the defence were browbeaten, silenced, and put down, or else interrupted by violent invectives against Baxter.

At one time the Lord Chief Justice exclaimed: "This is an old rogue, who hath poisoned the world with his Kidderminster doctrine. He encouraged all the women and maids to bring their bodkins and thimbles to carry on war against the King of ever blessed memory. An old schismatical knave! A hypocritical villain!"

By and by he called Baxter "an old blockhead, an unthankful villain, a conceited, stubborn, fanatical dog. Hang him!" he said, "this one old fellow hath cast more reproaches on the constitution and discipline of our Church than will be wiped off for this hundred years. But I'll handle him for it, for he deserves to be whipped through the city."

Shortly afterwards, when Baxter began to say a few words on his own behalf, Jeffreys stopped him, crying out, "Richard, Richard, dost thou think we'll hear thee poison the Court? Richard, thou art an old fellow, an old knave; thou hast written books enough to load a cart, every one as full of sedition, I might say treason, as an egg is full of meat. Hadst thou been whipped out of thy writing trade forty years ago, it had been happy. Thou pretendest to be a preacher of the gospel of peace, and thou hast one foot in the grave: it is time for thee to think what kind of an account thou intendest to give. But leave thee to thyself and I see thou wilt go on as thou hast begun; but, by the grace of God, I will look after thee. I know thou hast a mighty party, and I see a great many of the brotherhood in corners, waiting to see what will become of this mighty dove; but, by the grace of God Almighty, I'll crush you all! Come, what do you say for yourself, you old knave? Come, speak up!"

All this, and much more of the same kind, and even worse, went on at Baxter's trial. The extracts I have given form but a small portion of the whole account.

It is needless to say, that in such a court as this Baxter was at once found guilty. He was fined five hundred marks, which it was known he could not pay; condemned to lie in prison till he paid it, and bound over to good behaviour for seven years. And the issue of the matter was, that this poor, old, diseased, childless widower, of threescore years and ten, lay for two years in Southwark gaol!

It is needless, I hope, to remark in this present century that such a trial as this was a disgrace to the judicial bench of England, and a still greater disgrace to those persons with whom the information originated, understood commonly to have been Sherlock and L'Estrange. Thank God! I trust England, at any rate, has bid a long farewell to such trials as these, whatever may be done in other lands! Wretched, indeed, is that country where low, sneaking informers are encouraged; where the terrors of the law are directed more against holiness, and Scriptural religion, and freedom of thought, than against vice and immorality; and where the seat of justice is used for the advancement of political purposes, or the gratification of petty ecclesiastical spite!

But it is right that we should know that under all this foul injustice and persecution, Baxter's grace and patience never failed him. "These things," he said, in Westminster Hall, "will surely be understood one day, what fools one sort of Protestants are made to prosecute the other." When he was reviled, he reviled not again. He returned blessing for cursing, and prayer for ill-usage. Few martyrs have ever glorified God so much in their one day's fire as Richard Baxter did for twenty years under the ill-usage of so-called Protestants! Once more, I say, have I not a right to tell you such a man as this deserves to be remembered? Such a man surely deserves to be praised.

And now I hope I have proved my case. I trust it will be allowed that there are men who lived in times long gone by whose character it is useful to review, and that Baxter is undeniably one of them: a real man—a true spiritual hero.

I do not ask men to regard him as a perfect and faultless being, any more than Cranmer, or Calvin, or Knox, or Wesley. I do not at all defend some of Baxter's doctrinal statements. He tried to systematise things which cannot be systematised, and he failed. You will not find such a clear, full gospel in his writings as in those of Owen, and Bridge, and Traill. I do not think he was always right in his judgment. I regard his refusal of a bishopric as a huge mistake. By that refusal he rejected a glorious opportunity of doing good. Had Baxter been on the episcopal bench, and in the House of Lords, I do not believe the Act of Uniformity would ever have passed.

But in a world like this we must take true Christians as they are, and be thankful for what they are. It is not given to mortal man to be faultless. Take Baxter for all together, and there are few English ministers of the gospel whose names deserve to stand higher than his. Some have excelled him in some gifts, and some in others. But it is seldom that so many gifts are to be found united in one man as they are in Baxter. Eminent personal holiness, amazing power as a preacher, unrivalled pastoral skill, indefatigable diligence as a writer, meekness and patience under undeserved persecution— all meet together in the character of this one man. Let us place him high in our list of great and good men. Let us give him the honour he deserves. It is no small thing to be the fellow-countryman of Richard Baxter.

Our Debt to Baxter and the Puritans

And here let me remark that few bodies of men are under greater obligation to Baxter and his friends than the members of voluntary religious societies in the present day.

We are allowed to associate together upon Evangelical principles and for religious ends, and no one hinders us. We are allowed to meet in large numbers, and take sweet counsel with one another, and strengthen one another's hands in the service of Christ, and no one interferes to prevent us. We are allowed to assemble for devotional purposes, to read the word of God, and stir one another up to perseverance in the faith, and no one dares to prohibit us. How great are all these privileges! How incalculable the benefit of union, conference, sympathy, and encouragement to Christians who are voyaging over the stormy waters of this evil world, and trying to do good. Blessed is the labour of those by whose care and attention these societies are kept together! They are sowing precious seed. They may sow with much toil and discouragement, but they may be sure they are sowing seed which shall yet bear fruit after many days.

But never let us forget to whom we are indebted for all this liberty of conference and association which we enjoy. Never let us forget that there was a time when informers would have tracked all our steps—when constables and soldiers would have rudely broken up our gatherings at Exeter Hall, and when our proceedings would have entailed upon us pains, penalties, fines, and imprisonments. Never let us forget that the happy and profitable freedom which we enjoy was only won by long continued and intense struggles, by the blood and sufferings of noble-minded men, of whom the world was not worthy; and never forget that the men who won this freedom for us were those much-abused men—the Puritans.

Yes! We all owe a debt to the Puritans, which I trust we shall never refuse to acknowledge. We live in days when many are disposed to run them down. As we travel through life, we often hear them derided and abused as seditious, rebellious levellers in the things of Caesar, and ignorant, fanatical, hypocritical enthusiasts in the things of God. We often hear some conceited stripling fresh from college, puffed up with new-fledged views of what he calls "apostolical succession," and proud of a little official authority, depreciating and sneering at the Puritans as men alike destitute of learning and true religion, while, in reality he is scarcely worthy to sit at their feet and carry their books. To all such calumnies and false statements, I trust we shall never give heed.

Let us settle it down in our minds that for sound doctrine, spirituality, and learning combined, the Puritans stand at the head of English divines. With all their faults, weaknesses, and defects, they alone kept the lamp of pure, Evangelical religion burning in this country in the times of the Stuarts—they alone prevented Laud's Popish inclinations carrying England back into the arms of Rome. It was they who fought the battle of religious freedom, of which we are reaping such fruits. It was they who crushed the wretched spirit of inquisitorial persecution which misguided High Churchmen tried to introduce into this land.

Let us give them the honour they deserve. Let us suffer no man to speak lightly of them in our presence. Let us remember our obligations to them, reverence their memory, stand up boldly for their reputation, and never be afraid to plead their cause. It is the cause of pure, Evangelical religion. It is the cause of an open Bible and liberty to meet, and read, and pray together. It is the cause of liberty of conscience. All these are bound up with Baxter and the Puritans. Let us remember this, and give them their due.

Baxter's Death

Baxter's last days were almost as remarkable as any in his life. He went down to his grave as calmly and peacefully as the setting sun in summer. His death-bed was a glorious death-bed indeed.

I like to know how great men die. I am not satisfied with knowing that men are great Christians in the plenitude of riches and honour. I want to know whether they were great in view of the tomb. I do not want merely to know how men meet Kings and Bishops and Parliaments; I want to know how they meet the king of terrors, and how they feel in the prospect of standing before the King of kings. I suspect that greatness which forsakes a man at last. I like to know how great men die, and I must be allowed to dwell for a few moments upon Baxter's death.

Few death-beds, perhaps, were ever more truly instructive than that of this good old Puritan. His friend, Dr. Bates, has given a full description of it, and I think a few facts drawn from it may prove a suitable conclusion to this biography.

Baxter's last illness found him quietly living in Charterhouse Square, close to the meeting-house of his friend, Dr. Sylvester. Here for the four years preceding his death, he was allowed to enjoy great quietness. The liberty of preaching the things concerning the Lord Jesus Christ, no man forbidding him, was at length fully conceded. "Here," says Dr. Calamy, "he used to preach with great freedom about another world, like one that had been there, and was come as a sort of express to make a report of it." The storm of persecution was at length over. The winds and waves that had so long burst over him were at last lulled. The saintly old Puritan was mercifully allowed to go down to the banks of Jordan in a great calm.

He continued to preach so long, notwithstanding his wasted body, that the last time he almost died in the pulpit. When disease compelled him to give over his beloved work, and take to his dying bed, it found him the same man that he had been for fifty years. His last hours were spent in preparing others and himself to meet God. He said to the friends who visited him, "You come hither to learn to die. I am not the only person that must go this way. Have a care of this vain, deceitful world, and the lust of the flesh. Be sure you choose God for your portion, heaven for your home, God's glory for your end, God's Word for your rule, and then you need never fear but we shall meet again with comfort."

Never was penitent sinner more humble, and never was sincere believer more calm and comfortable. He said, "God may justly condemn me for the best duty I ever did; and all my hopes are from the free mercy of God in Christ." He had often said before, "I can more readily believe that God will forgive me, than I can forgive myself" (Acts 8:2).

After a slumber, he waked, saying, "I shall rest from my labours." A minister present said, "And your works will follow you." He replied, "No works; I will leave out works, if God will grant me the other." When a friend comforted him with the remembrance of the good many had received from his writings, he replied, "I was but a pen in God's hand, and what praise is due to a pen?"

When extremity of pain made him long for death, he would check himself and say, "It is not fit for me to prescribe: when Thou wilt—what Thou wilt—how Thou wilt!" Being in great anguish, he said, "How unsearchable are His ways!" and then he said to his friends, "Do not think the worse of religion for what you see me suffer."

Being often asked by his friend how it was with his inward man, he replied, "I have a well-grounded assurance of my eternal happiness, and great peace and comfort within; but it is my trouble that I cannot triumphantly express it, by reason of extreme pain." He added, "Flesh must perish, and we must feel the perishing; and though my judgment submit, sense will make me groan."

Being asked by a nobleman whether he had great joy from his believing apprehension of the invisible state, he replied, "What else, think you, Christianity serves for?" And then he added, "that the consideration of the Deity, in His glory and greatness, was too high for our thoughts; but the consideration of the Son of God in our nature and of the saints in heaven whom we knew and loved, did much sweeten and familiarise heaven to him." The description of heaven in the 12th chapter of Hebrews, beginning with the "innumerable company of angels," and ending with "Jesus the Mediator, and the blood of sprinkling," was very comfortable to him. "That scripture," he said, "deserves a thousand thousand thoughts!" And then he added, "Oh, how comfortable is that promise, 'Eye has not seen, nor ear heard, neither hath it entered into the heart of man to conceive, the things God hath laid up for them that love Him!'"

At another time he said, that "he found great comfort and sweetness in repeating the words of the Lord's Prayer, and was sorry that some good men were prejudiced against the use of it; for there were all necessary petitions for soul and body contained in it."

He gave excellent counsel to young ministers who visited him on his deathbed. He used to pray earnestly "that God would bless their labours, and make them very successful in converting many souls to Christ." He expressed great joy in the hope that God would do a great deal of good by them, and that they would be of moderate, peaceful spirits.

He did not forget the world he was leaving. He frequently prayed "that God would be merciful to this miserable, distracted world; and that he would preserve his Church and interest in it."

He advised his friends "to beware of self-conceitedness, as a sin likely to ruin this nation." Being asked at the same time whether he had altered his mind in controversial points, he replied, "Those that please may know my mind in my writings. What I have done was not for my own reputation, but the glory of God."

The day before he died, Dr. Bates visited him; and on his saying some words of comfort, he replied, "I have pain: there is no arguing against sense; but I have peace: I have peace!" Bates told him he was going to his long desired home. He answered, "I believe: I believe." He expressed great willingness to die. During his sickness, when the question was asked how he did, his reply was, "Almost well!" or else, "Better than I deserve to be, but not so well as I hope to be." His last words were addressed to Dr. Sylvester, "The Lord teach you how to die".

On Tuesday, the 8th of December 1691, Baxter's warfare was accomplished; and at length he entered what he had so beautifully described—"the saint's everlasting rest."

He was buried at Christchurch, amidst the tears of many who knew his worth, if the world and the Established Church of that day did not. The funeral was that kind of funeral which is above all in real honour: "devout men carried him to his grave, and made great lamentation over him" (Acts 8:2).

He left no family, but he left behind him hundreds of spiritual sons and daughters. He left works which are still owned by God in every part of the world to the awakening and edification of immortal souls. Thousands, I doubt not, will stand up in the morning of the resurrection, and thank God for the grace and gifts bestowed on the old Puritan of Shropshire. He left a name which must always be dear to every lover of holiness, and every friend of religious liberty. No Englishman, perhaps, ever exemplified the one, or promoted the other, more truly and really than did Richard Baxter.

Let me conclude by quoting the last paragraph of Dr. Bates' funeral sermon on the occasion of Baxter's death:

> *Blessed be the gracious God, that he was pleased to prolong the life of his servant, so useful and beneficial to the world, to a full age, and that he brought him slowly and safely to heaven. I shall conclude this account with my own deliberate wish: May I live the short remainder of my life as entirely to the glory of God as he lived; and when I shall come to the period of my life, may I die in the same blessed peace wherein he died; may I be with him in the kingdom of light and love for ever.*

2. Archbishop Laud

William Laud, Archbishop of Canterbury, was beheaded on Tower Hill, London, in the year 1645. He was one of five Archbishops in historical times who died violent deaths. Alphege was killed by the Danes in 1009, in Ethelred's reign. Thomas à Becket was suddenly murdered in Canterbury Cathedral, in the reign of Henry II. Simon Sudbury was beheaded by Wat Tyler, in the reign of Richard II. Cranmer was burned by Papists at Oxford, in the days of Queen Mary. Laud alone died by Protestant hands, in Charles the First's time, at the beginning of the Long Parliament.

Now what have we got to do with Archbishop Laud? Many, I venture to suspect, are ready to ask that question. Two centuries have passed away since Laud died. Steam, electricity, railways, free trade, reform, education, science, have changed everything in England. Why rake up the melancholy story of a barbarous deed done in semi-barbarous times? What is Laud to us, or we to Laud, that we need trouble ourselves with him and his history?

Questions like these, I make bold to say, are rather short-sighted and inconsiderate. History, it has been wisely said, is "philosophy teaching by examples" and of no history is that saying so true as of the history of the Church. History, it has again been said, "has a strange tendency to repeat itself," and a close study of the history of the past will help us greatly to conjecture what will happen in the future. It is my firm belief that we have a great deal to do with Laud, and that a knowledge of Laud's times is of great importance in the present day. I will go further. I believe that the history of Laud throws broad and clear light on the present position of the Church of England.

I must begin by throwing myself on the kind indulgence of my readers, and soliciting a large measure of patience and consideration. My subject is an historical one. Few men, except Froude and Macaulay, can make history anything but dry and dull. When king Ahasuerus could not sleep, the chronicles, or history of his own times, were read to him (Esther 6:1). My subject, moreover, is peculiarly surrounded with difficulties. Never was there a character so differently estimated as that of Laud. According to some, he was a Papist and a monster of iniquity; according to others, he was a blessed martyr and an angel of light. Between the violent abuse of Prynne, on the one hand, and the preposterous admiration of Heylin, Wharton, Lawson, and even Le Bas, on the other, it is extremely hard to find out the truth. In short, the subject is a tangled skein, and at this distance of time it is difficult to unravel it.

Nevertheless, I shall boldly try to set before my readers "the thing as it is." After careful investigation my own mind is thoroughly made up. I hold that, wittingly or unwittingly, meaningly or unmeaningly, intentionally or unintentionally, Laud did more harm to the Church of England than any Churchman that ever lived. He inflicted a wound that will never be healed; he worked mischief that will never be repaired.

Laud was born in the year 1573, about thirty-five years after the beginning of the Reformation, in the middle of Queen Elizabeth's reign, and came forward as a public man about the time of James the First's accession, in 1603. I ask particular attention to these dates. A moment's reflection will show that he appeared on the stage of English Church history at a most critical period: that is to say, within the first seventy-five years after the commencement of the glorious English Reformation.

Seventy-five years only! How short a time that seems! Yet how many events of deepest interest to us all were crowded into that period. Within those seventy-five years the seed of Protestantism was first sown by Henry the Eighth, though I fully admit from low, carnal, and worldly motives. Then came the short but glorious reign of Edward the Sixth, when the tender plant grew with hot-bed rapidity under the fostering care of Cranmer, Ridley, Latimer, and Hooper. Then came the bloody reign of Mary, when it was cut down to the very ground by the ferocious proceedings of Bonner and Gardiner. Then came the happy reaction, on Elizabeth's accession to the throne, and the final re-establishment of the Church of England on the basis which it now occupies.

But even Elizabethan times, I am sorry to say, were not times of unmixed good to the Church of England. The truth must be spoken on this point. In our thankfulness for the good Elizabeth did, we are rather apt to overlook the harm which was done in her reign. Things were left undone that ought to have been done, and done that ought not to have been done. Partly from the Queen's characteristic Tudor love of power, and jealousy of the Bishops, and partly from her anxious desire to conciliate and win over the Papists, the work of the Reformation was not carried forward so energetically as it might have been.

The Zurich letters, published by the Parker Society, contain many hints about this. If Jewel and his companions had not been incessantly thwarted and hampered by royal interference, our Church's worship and organization would probably have been made far better than it is. If Grindal had not been snubbed and stopped in the matter of the "prophesyings," the English clergy would have been a far better body than they were. His letter to the Queen on that painful occasion deserves unmixed admiration. Partly again, from the universal ignorance of toleration which prevailed among all parties, conscientious men were often persecuted for trifling offences, and the ground was prepared for an abundant crop of dissent in after times. Fuller, the historian, records some curious correspondence between Cecil, and other Privy Councillors, and Archbishop Whitgift, on this subject. I am sorry to appear to depreciate Elizabeth. But truth is truth, and ought to be known; and we cannot properly understand Laud, unless we understand the times which immediately preceded him.[24]

One bright point, however, should never be forgotten in estimating the reign of Elizabeth. The standard of doctrine in the Church of England was sound, clear, Scriptural, and unmistakable. Rightly or wrongly, nothing was tolerated in pulpits which was not thoroughly Protestant, and thoroughly agreeable to all the *Thirty-nine Articles*. A clergyman who preached up the real presence of Christ's body and blood, under the forms of bread and wine in the sacrament, or recommended the practice of private confession to a priest, or advocated prayer to the Virgin Mary, or elevated the consecrated elements over his head in the Lord's Supper and adored them, or taught a gross, *opus operatum* view of baptismal regeneration, or publicly denied the doctrine of predestination, or imputed righteousness, or justification by faith, or reviled the memory of Cranmer, Ridley, and Latimer, or called Edward the Sixth "a young tiger-cub," or sneered at the Articles as "forty stripes save one," or recommended reunion with the Church of Rome, or hesitated to call the Pope Antichrist, such a man, I say boldly, unless he had been a very insignificant person, would have had a very hard time of it in the days of Good Queen Bess! The "powers that be" would have come down upon him like a thunderbolt. These were subjects which were hardly even allowed to be controverted; you must either hold strong Protestant views about them, or hold your tongue.

In short, however faulty and deficient in many things, the Church of England in Queen Elizabeth's time was in theory downright Protestant and Evangelical. Weak, by reason of her infancy, the Church may have been; defective in many points, judged by our light, no doubt she was; marred and damaged by stupid intolerance she certainly was; but at no period was her general standard of doctrine so Scriptural and so Protestant as in the days of Elizabeth. Men and women were yet alive who had seen Rogers and Brad-

---

[24] The reader who cares to look into this subject will find a remarkable letter to Whitgift in favour of the persecuted Nonconformists, dated 1583, and signed by Burleigh, Warwick, Howard, Hatton, Shrewsbury, Leicester, Croft, Walsingham—eight leading privy councillors. See Fuller's *Church History*, Volume 3, page 37 (Tegg's Edition).

ford burned in Smithfield, who had heard old Latimer say to Ridley at the stake, "Courage, we shall light a candle which shall never be extinguished," who had watched gallant Hooper patiently agonizing in the fire for three quarters of an hour under the shadow of Gloucester Cathedral. Men and women in England had not yet forgotten these things. There was a widespread feeling that Popery was a false religion, and Protestantism was God's truth; that Popish doctrine in every shape was to be held in abhorrence, and that Reformation doctrines ought never to be given up. All classes held this, with very few exceptions, from the statesman in the Council Chamber down to the apprentice-boy in the shop. In short, the days of Elizabeth, with all their faults, were Protestant days. The nation was professedly a Protestant nation, and gloried in the name. This is a point which ought never to be forgotten. Well would it have been for our country if Elizabethan Protestantism had been as real and deep as it seemed.

Such were the critical times in which William Laud was allowed by God to come forward, and become a power in England. Such was the state of things which he found in our Church. How he deliberately set himself to oppose the current theology of his day, how he "practised and prospered" for forty years, how he worked night and day to compass his ends, as "thorough" as Lord Strafford in driving on toward his mark, how he rallied round him in an Arminian cave of Adullam (cf. 1 Samuel 22:1-2) every Churchman who was discontented with the doctrines of the Reformation, how he gradually leavened our Church with a distaste for true Protestantism, and a dislike for what he was pleased to call "Calvinism," how, even after ruining Church and State by his policy, he left behind him a school of Churchmen which has done immense harm to our Church—all these are historical facts, which would fill a volume if fully described. In a chapter like the present they can only be briefly pointed out. The utmost that I shall attempt to do is to supply a bare outline of Laud's life, and a brief estimate of his character, and to show the policy he had in view, the manner in which he carried it out, and the consequences to which it led. A few practical lessons for ourselves will then form a fitting conclusion to the whole.

Laud's early life

William Laud was born at Reading in the year 1573, and was the son of respectable parents of the middle class. He received his early education at the Grammar School of his native town, and in the year 1589 entered St. John's College, Oxford. Little is known of his boyhood and youth, except that he was physically weak and puny, but intellectually vigorous, and a young man of untiring industry and application. His master at Reading School was so convinced from observation that he was one of those boys who are sure to rise in the world, that he used to say, "When you are a great little man, remember Reading School."

At Oxford he gradually, though slowly, made himself known and felt. In 1593 he was elected Fellow of his College, and after losing two years from illness was made Master of Arts in 1598, and ordained Deacon by Young, Bishop of Rochester, in 1600, and Priest in 1601.

Of his ways and pursuits during the first ten years of his Oxford life very little is known, except the suspicious fact that Buckeridge, a notoriously unsound divine, was his tutor. It is evident that he was a careful observer of the times, and one who thought for himself. Even at the period of his ordination he had already taken up a theological line of his own. Bishop Young is said to have observed that his studies had not been confined to the ordinary system of Geneva, but that his divinity was built "on the noble foundation of the Fathers, the councils, and the ecclesiastical historians." Praise like this is suspicious. When a man makes an idol of Fathers and councils, and disparages the theology of the Reformation, we may be sure there is a screw loose in his theology.

Wood, the author of *Athenæ Oxonienses*, says that, even in his first ten years at Oxford, he was esteemed "a very forward, confident, and zealous man." Put together Bishop Young's and Wood's remarks, and you have the first ingredients of a very dangerous Churchman. I venture the conjecture, that these eleven quiet years at St. John's, Oxford were the seed-time of all the mischief that Laud ever did, and fixed the unhappy bias which characterized his whole career.

His appointment to read a divinity lecture at St. John's in 1602 was the first occasion when Laud came forward as the opponent of popular Protestantism, and the avowed advocate of a new style of theology. The precise nature of the opinions he propounded is not recorded, but according to Heylin it was something like "the perpetual visibility of the Church of Christ, derived from the Apostles to the Church of Rome, and continued in that Church until the Reformation." What it was that he said exactly we do not know; but it is pretty clear that he took up ground about the Church of Rome which was quite opposed to the views of the Homilies, Jewel, and the Reformers, and most distasteful to the thorough Protestants of the University.

The immediate result was that the lecturer came into collision with no less a person than Dr. George Abbot, then Vice-Chancellor of Oxford, Head of University College, and afterwards Archbishop of Canterbury—a man of great ability and deservedly high character. The after-consequences were that from that day forward Abbot regarded Laud as a dangerous man, and Laud became marked and known as a very lukewarm Protestant, if not a friend of Popery, and an open enemy to the pure gospel of Christ.

After serving the office of Proctor in 1603, Laud took his degree as Bachelor of Divinity in 1604. The propositions he undertook to defend in his exercises for that degree, supplied additional proof of his theological tendencies and increased the suspicion with which he was regarded. According to his biographers he maintained, first, the "necessity of baptism;" and secondly, that "there could be no true Church without diocesan Bishops." The precise nature of his statements, again, is not known; but it is evident, from the stir which the exercises made, that they were thought unscriptural and unsound hitherto by Protestant Churchmen. It seems most probable that, like the promoters of the "Tracts for the Times," he maintained apostolical succession and baptismal regeneration. Whatever it was that he said, it is a fact that he was severely attacked by Dr. Holland, Rector of Exeter, who was at that time Regius Professor of Divinity. As usual, nothing came of the attack, and Laud held his ground. Moral evidence of a man's theological unsoundness, and legal proof of it, are totally different things.

After damaging himself seriously, in 1605, by countenancing and solemnizing a most discreditable marriage between the earl of Essex and Lady Rich, Laud got into another theological difficulty at Oxford in 1606. He delivered a sermon in St. Mary's of such a Romish tendency, that he was called in question for it by Dr. Airay, Provost of Queen's, at that time Vice-Chancellor. Again we are left in ignorance of the nature of the sermon, and again we only know that, as usual, Laud contrived to escape public censure. But, like many others in a similar position, though not legally condemned, he established a strong impression in many minds that he was a thoroughly unsound divine, and deeply tainted with Romanizing opinions. Such, in short, was the scandal raised by this discourse, that the famous Joseph Hall, afterwards Bishop of Norwich, took occasion to address a remarkable letter of expostulation to the preacher, which, as an indication of the estimate then made of Laud's character, deserves quoting at length. He says:—

> *I would I knew where to find you; then I could tell how to take direct aim. Whereas now I must pore and conjecture. Today you are in the tents of the Romanists, tomorrow in ours, the next day between both and against both. Our adversaries think you ours. We think you theirs. Your conscience finds you with both and neither. I flatter you not. This, of course, is the worst of all tempers. Heat and cold have their uses. Lukewarmness is good for nothing, but to trouble the stomach. Those that are spiritually hot find acceptation. Those that are stark cold have lesser reckoning. The mean between both is much worse, as it comes nearer to good and yet attains it not. How long will you be in this indifferency?*
>
> *Resolve one way, and know at last what you do hold, what you should. Cast off either your wings or your teeth; and, casting off this bat-like nature, be either a bird or a beast. To die wavering or uncertain, yourself will grant fearful. If you must settle, when begin you? If you*

must begin, why not now? It is dangerous deferring that whose want is deadly, and whose opportunity is doubtful. God crieth with Jehu, 'Who is on my side? Who?' [2 Kings 9:32] Look at last out of your window to Him, and in a resolute courage cast down the Jezebel that hath bewitched you. Is there any impediment which delay will abate? Is there any which a just answer cannot remove? If you would rather waver, who can settle you? But if you love not inconstancy, tell us why you stagger? Be plain, or else you will never be firm.[25]

In 1607, in the thirty-fourth year of his age, Laud began at last to climb the ladder of ecclesiastical preferment. A man of his stamp, who had come forward as an opponent of Protestant and Evangelical theology, was sure not to lack patrons. Such men "speak of the world, and the world heareth them" (1 John 4:5). In fact from this date, until he became a Bishop, I can hardly find three years in which Laud did not obtain some piece of preferment. In 1607 he was made Vicar of Stamford, in Northamptonshire; in 1608, Rector of North Kibworth, in Leicestershire, and Chaplain to Neile, Bishop of Rochester; in 1609, Rector of West Tilbury, Essex; in 1610, Rector of Cuckstone, Kent, and then of Norton in the same county; in 1611, President of St. John's College, Oxford, and Chaplain to the King; in 1614, Prebendary of Buckden, in the Diocese of Lincoln; in 1615, Archdeacon of Huntingdon; in 1616, Dean of Gloucester; in 1618, Rector of Ibstock in Leicestershire; in 1620, Canon of Westminster; and in 1622, Rector of Crick, in Northamptonshire.[26]

Such a number of successive preferments probably were never heaped on one man in an equal space, of time! How many of them he held at once I am unable to ascertain. What he did at his various livings, whether he resided much, whether he preached much, whether he left any spiritual marks for good, are all points about which no information remains. Except the fact that in each parish he always assigned an annual pension to twelve poor persons, laid aside one-fifth of his income for charitable

---

25 Hall's *Letters*, Decade 3, Letter 5.

26 Laud appears to have taken the living of Crick after he became Bishop of St. David's. See his *Diary*.

purposes, put the glebe house in repair, and saw that the church was supplied with becoming furniture, I can find nothing recorded. As to any evangelistic work, bearing fruit in men's souls, in Stamford, North Kibworth, West Tilbury, Cuckstone, Norton, Ibstock, or Crick, we are left entirely in the dark. In truth, there is no evidence that work of this kind was at any time much in Laud's line.

Two public incidents in Laud's life during the thirteen years between 1607 and 1620 deserve special notice. One throws strong light on the estimate which was formed of him in the place where he was best known—the University of Oxford; the other supplies a striking example of the thorough unbending style in which he drove on his own schemes for unprotestantizing the Church of England, and thrust them down men's throats in the face of opposition.

The first of these incidents is the public rebuke which he received at Oxford, in consequence of a sermon which he preached before the University on Shrove Tuesday, 1614. This sermon contained matter so offensive to Protestant Churchmen, that the Vice-Chancellor, Robert Abbot, brother of the Archbishop of Canterbury, and afterwards Bishop of Salisbury, a man of great piety and learning, thought fit to give it a public answer the following Easter Sunday, in a sermon at St. Mary's.

The following passage from Abbot's sermon is highly important, as showing what Laud's theological opinions really were. "Some men," said Abbot in his sermon,

> are partly *Romish* and partly *English*, as occasion serves them; so that a man may say unto them, "Art thou for us or for our adversaries?" They are men who under pretence of truth, and preaching against the Puritans, strike at the heart and root of the faith and religion now established among us. This preaching against the Puritans was the practice of Parsons and Campian the Jesuits, when they came into England to seduce young students. When many of them were afraid to lose their places, if they should professedly be thus, the counsel they then gave them was that they should speak freely against the Puritans,

and that would suffice. These men cannot plead that they are only accounted Papists because they speak against the Puritans, but because they speak nothing against the Papists. If they do at any time speak anything against the Papists, they do but beat about the bush; and that but softly, for fear of awakening and disquieting the birds that are in it. They speak nothing but that wherein one Papist will speak against another, or against equivocations and the Pope's temporal authority, and the like; and perhaps, against some of their blasphemous opinion. But on the points of free-will, justification, concupiscence being sin after baptism, inherent righteousness, and certainty of salvation, the Papists beyond the sea can say they are wholly theirs, and the recusants at home make their brags of them. And in all things they keep so near the brink, that upon any occasion they may step over to them.

I make no comment on this passage: it speaks for itself. My readers will probably agree with me, that it would have been well if Vice-Chancellors of Oxford had always spoken as plainly and faithfully as Robert Abbot, and that Laud is not the only person who has required such public rebuke to be given. I only ask then to mark carefully the charges against Laud which the passage contains. It shows clearly and unmistakably what was the Oxford estimate, and the real nature of Laud's theology.

The other incident to which I ask attention in this period of Laud's life is the collision which took place between him and the Bishop of Gloucester, immediately after his appointment to the Deanery of Gloucester, in the year 1616. His very first act, on taking office in the Cathedral, was to remove the communion table from the place where it had long stood, in the midst of the choir, to the wall at the east end, where he ordered it to stand altar-wise. The change may seem a trifling one to many now, accustomed, as we have been, for 200 years, to see the table in this position; but a right understanding of the old position of the table throws broad light on the famous expression, "On the north side." The change appeared a very serious matter to all good Protestants in 1616, as tending to bring back the Papal notion of an altar, and to encourage the idea of a sacrifice, and a priest, and the Mass, in the Lord's Supper.

The people of Gloucester were of all English citizens the least likely to approve the slightest appearance of a leaning towards Popery. They had not forgotten good Bishop Hooper, and the doctrine he had so often preached about the Lord's Supper before his martyrdom. Miles Smith, the Bishop of Gloucester, a holy and learned man, and one of the leading translators of the Authorised version of the Bible, was more offended by the change than any one, and declared if it was carried into effect he would never enter the Cathedral again. But none of these things moved Laud; in spite of Bishop and people the table was moved. The Dean had his own way. The Bishop was publicly set at nought, and never entered his own Cathedral again, though living within fifty yards of it, until the day of his death, in 1624. The feelings of the Protestant people of Gloucester were deeply wounded. It is a striking and significant fact that afterwards, when the Commonwealth wars began, no place resisted the Cavaliers and fought for Parliament so stubbornly as this very city of Gloucester!

This unhappy transaction requires little comment from me. Like the affair of Abbot's sermon, however, it gives another insight into Laud's character. It shows him determined to carry out his own views without regard to the offence they might give to the feelings of Protestant Churchmen. It shows him, like many in modern times, perfectly indifferent to his Bishop's wishes and opinions the very moment they ran counter to his own. Here is the very man who preached up Apostolical Succession at Oxford, flying in the face of a venerable Bishop, and trampling contemptuously on his conscientious scruples! It shows him, above all, beginning his official duties in a public position, by making a great and suspicious stir about the sacrament of the Lord's Supper, and attaching an ominous importance to the precise position of the Lord's Table. Need I remind many of my readers, that the first step of the whole Tractarian movement was exactly in the same direction? To exalt the Lord's Supper into a position neither warranted by the Bible, the Articles, nor the Prayer Book, and to invest the Lord's Table and all around it with a superstitious sanctity—these were among the first lessons taught by that school of which so many scholars have passed over to the Church of Rome. "I speak as to wise men; judge ye what I say."²⁷

In 1621, after five years at Gloucester Deanery, Laud's ambition was once more gratified, and his power of mischief greatly increased, by his elevation to the bench as Bishop of St. David's. To thrust upon the bench, once filled by Latimer and Jewel, a man who had been publicly opposed by three Vice-Chancellors and a Regius Professor of Divinity, required of course no small influence and exertion. Laud's friends were found equal to the occasion. For the appointment, he was mainly indebted to the Marquis of Buckingham, and to Williams, the well-known Bishop of Lincoln. King James, at any rate, seems to have given a very unwilling consent to his nomination. Partly, no doubt, from the character which Laud had notoriously obtained as a very lukewarm Protestant; partly from the open distrust with which Abbot, Archbishop of Canterbury, regarded him; and partly from a certain shrewdness in discerning unsound doctrine, the King raised serious objections to Laud being made a Bishop. The conversation on the subject between his majesty and Bishop Williams, preserved by Hackett in his life of Williams, is a very curious one, and shows plainly that the British Solomon (as people called James) was not quite such a fool as he was often thought to be.

"'I keep Laud back,' said the king, 'from all place of rule and authority, because I find that he hath a restless spirit, and cannot see when matters are well; but loves to toss and change, and bring matters to a pitch of reformation floating in his own brain, which may endanger the steadfastness of that which is at a good pass, God be praised. I speak not at random: he hath made himself known to me to be such an one.'" To this Williams could only reply that Laud was "of a great and tractable wit, and

---

[27] What Laud really thought about the Lord's Table may be seen in a very painful extract from a speech afterwards delivered by him in the Star Chamber, on the occasion of the prosecution of Prynne in 1637. He there says, *"The altar"* (a word, we must remember, never used in the Prayer Book), *"the altar is the greatest place of God's residence upon earth. I say the greatest, yea, greater than the pulpit; for there it is, 'This is my body,' but in the pulpit it is, 'This is my word.' And a greater reverence, no doubt, is due to the body than to the word of our Lord; and so to the throne where His body is actually present, than to the seat where His word useth to be proclaimed."

would presently see the way to come out of his error." At last, wearied out by Williams' importunity, the King said, "Is there no way but you must carry it? Then take him to you: but on my soul, you will repent it;" and went away in a rage, using other words of fierce and ominous import.

How true a prophet the King was, and how bitterly Williams afterwards smarted under Laud's base ingratitude, are notorious historical facts. But this was the way, and this the ladder, by which Laud climbed to the episcopal bench in 1621, in the forty-eighth year of his age.[28]

We have now reached the period of Laud's life when his unhappy influence began to be felt most powerfully in every department of Church and State. For the next twenty years after 1621, his history is so intermixed with the history of every great movement in our country, that to go fully into it would be to overload my subject, and make a plain biographical paper a volume of history. I cannot pretend to do anything of the kind. The utmost I shall attempt to do is to supply the leading incidents of his story, and the dates at which they occurred.

Laud's ascent and fall

In 1622 I find he was appointed "Confessor" to the Duke of Buckingham. In 1626 he was made Bishop of Bath and Wells, and Dean of the Chapel Royal. In 1628 he became Bishop of London. In 1630 he became Chancellor of Oxford. In 1633 he rose to be Archbishop of Canterbury and Chancellor of Dublin University. In 1640 he began at last to fall from his high estate, and in 1641 he was committed to the Tower.

How he conducted himself throughout these last twenty years of his life—how he plunged into politics with as much energy as any layman, how he became the intimate friend of such men as Buckingham, Straf-

---

28 Hackett's story is corroborated by one told by Bishop Burnet. "I have heard," says Bishop Burnet, "my own father relate it from the mouth of old Sir William Armourer, who was of King James the First's court, being bred up from a page, that his Majesty, as Laud (then only Bishop of St. David's) walked by, but at some distance, took Prince Charles by the arm, and in his Scottish dialect said to him, 'Son, ken you yon knave Laud? He has a restless head: he'll ne'er ha' done till he has lost his own head and endangered yours.'"—*Memorials of Princess Sophia*, pages 54-55.

ford, Windebank, and others of doubtful character, how he contrived to get the reputation of having a hand in everything that went on both in Church and State, how he managed to make himself the most unpopular man in England, from the Isle of Wight to Berwick-on-Tweed, and from the Land's End to the North Foreland, how at last not a mistake could be made, either political or ecclesiastical, without the cry being raised, "Is not the hand of Laud in all this?"— all these things are duly recorded in the historians of the times. They are far too many, and would occupy too much time to be detailed here.

One general remark applies to all his career throughout these twenty years. He was always consistent, always the same, always in mischief, always playing the same game, always driving at the same end, always advocating the same theological principles, for which he had made himself notorious at Oxford. In 1622, before he had been a Bishop a year, I find him assisting in the issue of six royal injunctions to the Clergy, in which, among other things, it is ordered, "that no one, under the degree of a Bishop or Dean, shall preach on such deep points as predestination, or election, or the universality, efficacy, resistibility, or irresistibility of God's grace."

- In 1631 I find him procuring the suppression of an admirable association for buying up presentations and appointing good clergymen, mainly got up by the famous Dr. Gouge. The association was broken up, and the money subscribed was confiscated.

- In 1631 I find him consecrating the Church of St. Catherine Cree, London, with such superstitious ceremonies and idolatrous veneration of the Lord's Table and the elements of bread and wine, that he made everyone suppose he longed to re-introduce downright Popery.

- In 1632 I find him prosecuting Sherfield, Recorder of Salisbury, for breaking a painted window in St. Edmund's Church, Salisbury, which the vestry had ordered to be removed, and this with such savage severity that the unfortunate man was fined £1,000 by the Star Chamber.

- In 1633 I find him first offending the feelings of the nation about the Sabbath by reviving and republishing The Book of Sports, and then ungratefully trampling on the feelings of Williams, Bishop of Lincoln, by visiting his diocese as metropolitan, and opposing his known opinion about the Lord's Table.

- In 1634 I find him persecuting the French and Walloon congregations in London, and pressing the Irish Church only too successfully to give up its admirable Articles.

- In 1636 I find him preparing and sending down to Scotland the notorious Scotch liturgy, in which the Real Presence is as plainly taught as any Papist could wish, and setting all Scotland in a flame by attempting to introduce it in public worship.

- In 1637 I find him forbidding the migration to America of a large body of Puritans, among whom was the famous Oliver Cromwell, and compelling some of the very men, who afterwards upset Church and State, to remain in England against their will.

- In the same year I find him prosecuting Prynne, Burton, and Bastwick, for publishing violent writings, and actually punishing them with a fine of £5,000 each, imprisonment for life, and the hideous penalty of having their ears cut off.

- In 1640 I find him transgressing one of the first principles of our constitution by getting canons passed in Convocation without the consent of Parliament.

This list of monstrous follies might easily be increased. To enter into the particulars of them is, of course, impossible. For twenty years a petty warfare was kept up by him and his allies on the Episcopal bench against some of the holiest and best ministers of the land. The catalogue of famous men, who, at one time or another, during Laud's day of power, were prosecuted, silenced, fined, imprisoned, or driven to retire to the Continent, is a melancholy roll, and of itself speaks volumes. John Rogers, Daniel Rogers, Thomas Hooker, Dod, Hildersham, Ward, Cotton, Bridge, Ames, Sheppard, Burroughs, Greenhill, Calamy, Whateley, Wilkinson, Goodwin, were all men who had more divinity in their little fingers than Laud had in his whole body. Yet every one of them was visited with Laud's displeasure, and, in one way or another, disgracefully treated.

In short, the public came to the conclusion that Laud and his companions thought Puritanism a greater sin than open immorality, and trifling acts of nonconformity worse than breaking the ten commandments! It really came to this, that men said you might lie, or swear, or get drunk, and little notice would be taken; but to be a Puritan, or a Nonconformist, was to commit the unpardonable sin!

Never, I think, did mortal man labour so unceasingly to advance his own particular theological views as Laud, and never did any one seem so blind to the mischievous effects of his proceedings. Had half the zeal he displayed in snubbing Calvinists, persecuting Puritans, promoting Arminians, and making advances towards Rome, been shown by Grindal, Whitgift, and Abbot, in propagating Evangelical religion, it would have been a great blessing to the Church of England. Unhappily, we see in his case, as in many others, how much "wiser in their generation" the children of this world are than the children of light. Besides, untiring activity is far more often the characteristic of the friends of error than of the friends of truth. Pharisees, Jesuits, heresiarchs, in every age, will compass sea and land, and leave no stone unturned, to accomplish their ends, while the so-called Protestant soldier slumbers and sleeps. It was so in the days of Laud; I fear it is too much the case in the present day.

The end came at last. The patience of the English people was at length fairly exhausted. After a long and unseemly endeavour to govern without a parliament, that unhappy monarch, Charles the First, was obliged to summon the famous Long Parliament in 1640. From the very first meeting of the House of Commons, the Archbishop of Canterbury's doom was sealed. Hollis, Pym, Dering, and their companions, attacked Strafford and Laud without delay, and gave them no respite till they had brought them to the scaffold. The virulence of the attack made upon both these great officials, the singular unanimity with which the proceedings were carried on, the strong language which men of all parties, even quiet people like Lord Falkland, used in speaking of the Church of England, are all most curious facts, and should be studied in Rushworth's *Collections*, May's *History of the Long Parliament*, or Stoughton's *Church of the Civil Wars*. They all help to show the deep dissatisfaction which Laud's policy had long created in the mind of the public, and the intensity of the dislike with which he was personally regarded. Englishmen are notoriously slow to move, and curiously backward to resist constituted authority. When, therefore, Englishmen moved with such tremendous violence as the House of Commons moved against Laud, it is impossible not to feel that a very strong sense of long-standing grievances must have existed.

Laud was kept a prisoner from the 18th December 1640 to the 10th of January 1645, and the greater part of that time he was confined to the Tower. The articles laid to his charge were fourteen in number. In substance they were as follows (I copy Le Bas):—

1. That he had traitorously endeavoured to subvert the fundamental laws of the realm, and to persuade the King that he might levy money without the consent of Parliament.

2. That he had encouraged sermons and publications tending to the establishment of arbitrary power.

3. That he had interrupted and prevented the course of justice at Westminster Hall.

4. That he had traitorously and corruptly sold justice, and advised the King to sell judicial and other offices.

5. That he had surreptitiously caused a book of canons to be published without lawful authority, and had unlawfully enforced subscription to it.

6. That he had assumed a Papal and tyrannical power, both in eccle-

siastical and temporal matters.

7. That he had laboured to subvert God's true religion, and to introduce Papal superstition and idolatry.

8. That he had usurped the nomination to many ecclesiastical benefices, and promoted persons who were Popishly affected, or otherwise unsound in doctrine or corrupt in manners.

9. That he had committed the licensing of books to chaplains notoriously disaffected to the reformed religion.

10. That he had endeavoured to reconcile the Church of England to the Church of Rome, and held intelligence with priests and the Pope, and had permitted a Popish hierarchy to be established in this kingdom.

11. That he had silenced many godly ministers, hindered the preaching of God's Word, cherished profaneness and ignorance, and caused many of the King's subjects to forsake the country.

12. That he had endeavoured to raise discord between the Church of England and other Reformed Churches, and had oppressed the Dutch and French congregations in England.

13. That he had laboured to introduce innovations in religion and government into the kingdom of Scotland, and to stir up war between the two countries.

14. That to preserve himself from being questioned for these traitorous practices, he had laboured to divert the ancient course of parliamentary proceeding, and to incense the King against all Parliaments.

Such were the charges brought against the unfortunate Archbishop, and upon these, with the addition of ten minor articles, he was finally brought to trial in March 1644. It will be seen, by comparison of dates, that he lingered in prison for four years. It must have been a bitter time for the fallen Prelate! The execution of his friend Strafford, the battles of the civil war, the King's ill-success, and the imposition of a fine of £20,000 on himself, no doubt were not the least part of his sorrows. At one time, in 1643, a motion was actually made in the House of Commons that Laud should be transported, untried and unheard, to New England in America; and it is by no means quite clear that some of his enemies would not have been glad to get rid of him in this fashion. But the motion fell to the ground, and at length, in the autumn of 1644, he was finally placed on his trial.

Of the trial itself I shall say but little. It was perhaps as unfair and discreditable to English history as any State trial that figures in our chronicles. The prosecution was committed to Prynne, who was the virulent and bigoted personal enemy of the prisoner. Laud's own private papers and diary were seized and relentlessly used, and he had to defend himself under immense disadvantages. As the case went on, the evidence on many points was manifestly insufficient, and would never have satisfied a really fair and impartial court. Those who wish to read up the subject should study Prynne's own narrative of this trial, in a folio called *Canterbury's Doom*. But it is as clear as daylight that Laud's condemnation was a foregone conclusion with his judges. In spite of a defence which even Prynne admits was "full, gallant, and pithy," in spite of a conspicuous absence of legal proof that he had committed anything worthy of death—at length, after great delays, the Archbishop of Canterbury was found guilty and sentenced to die.

Of his execution at Tower Hill, on the 9th of January 1645, I shall also say little. The only favour shown him on this occasion was, that he was beheaded and not hanged. His demeanour on the scaffold was courageous, dignified, calm, and in every way honourable to him. His address before death was worthy of a better cause. In fact, you may say of him, as it was said of another, "Nothing in all his life became him so much as the leaving of it." That his execution was as much a judicial murder as that of Sir Thomas More or Cranmer, I feel no doubt at all: but I cannot for a moment admit that he deserves to be called a "martyr." It is the cause, not the amount of suffering, which makes the martyr. That Laud met his death bravely and gallantly, I fully admit: but I never can admit that he had done nothing to exasperate men's minds against him, or that he was wholly innocent of everything laid to his charge, or that he died in support of a good cause.

The real William Laud

We have now traced the life of Laud from his cradle to his grave. It only remains for me to point out the great and instructive lessons which his life appears to teach us, and the broad and clear light which it throws on the position of the Church of England at the present day. But before I do this, I wish to say a few words on three disputed points. These points are Laud's real character, his real policy and aims, and the real consequences of his policy. I am well aware that this is debatable ground. In walking over it I cannot expect that all will agree with me. But I give my opinion freely, and men must take it for what it is worth.

Laud's real character

His real character, then: What was it? What is the estimate that we ought to put on him? The answer, as is often the case, lies in my judgment between two extremes. Laud was neither so good nor so bad a man as he is often represented. To call him a saint, a martyr, an English Cyprian, on one side, is simply ridiculous. I can discover no warrant for such extravagant praise. To paint him as a monster of iniquity, and a child of the devil, on the other side, is equally absurd. The charge falls to the ground as "not proven."

Let us give him his due. He was not an immoral or a covetous man. Few archbishops seem to have spent so little on themselves, and to have given so largely and liberally of their substance to promote learning and to strengthen the material part of the Church of England. He was a zealous and earnest Churchman. No one can deny that he spent himself and was spent in the promotion of what he thought sound "Church Views," and conscientiously believed he was doing right. But earnestness alone, if not rightly directed, is a very mischievous thing. Experience abundantly proves that, in every age of the Church, well-meaning and conscientious men, when they are narrow-minded, short-sighted, ignorant of human nature, and obstinate, are the greatest causes of trouble. Never did man prove it so thoroughly as Laud.

He was not, I believe, a Jesuit or a Papist. His conference with Fisher, and his successful dealings with Chillingworth, completely negate that supposition. But to call him a sound Protestant Churchman is simply absurd. He never disguised his dislike of thorough Protestant theology, and laboured all his life to discourage it. The mere fact that he was twice offered a cardinal's hat by the Pope, after he became Archbishop of Canterbury, of itself speaks volumes. It shows the general impression that he made on the minds of foreigners.

That he was a spiritually-minded man, and really received the gospel of God's grace into his heart, is a point of which we have very scanty proofs. This is a delicate matter. God forbid that we should judge him! Yet it is vain to deny that there is an absence of anything like thoroughly Evangelical, experimental religion in his literary remains. There is a painful lack of anything really calculated to do good to hearts and souls. His seven sermons are poor things, and not worthy to be compared even with the discourses of men of his own school, like Andrews. His private *Diary* contains much superstition and weakness. His letters are not spiritual or striking. It is not too much to say that you will find more good divinity in ten pages of such men as his contemporaries, Usher, Davenant, Hall, and Sibbes, than in all the works of Laud.

The plain truth must be spoken. Laud was much more a political Churchman, an ecclesiastical Ahithophel, a zealous champion of his party, his cause, and his order, than a minister of Christ, a preacher of the gospel, a shepherd of souls. For the work of the former character he laid himself out entirely, and laboured in it night and day. For the work of the latter character he had no vocation, and gave himself no time. It was not work in his line. What he really was, and what he really felt personally in his heart of hearts, is a question which I cannot pretend to solve. The last day alone will declare it. In hope and charity I leave it alone.

Laud's real policy and aims

Laud's real policy next demands our attention. What was it? What was he driving at all his life? What did he want to do? What was his object and aim? I do not believe, with some, that he really desired to Romanize the Church of England, or meant and intended, if possible, to reunite it with the Church of Rome. I think those who say this go too far, and have no sufficient ground for their assertions. But I decidedly think, that what he did labour to effect was just as dangerous, and would sooner or later have brought back downright Popery, no matter what Laud meant or intended. I believe that Laud's grand idea was to make the Church of England less Protestant, less Calvinistic, less Evangelical, than it was when he found it. I believe he thought that our excellent Reformers had gone too far—that the clock ought to be put back a good deal. I believe his favourite theory was, that we ought to occupy a medium position between the Reformation on the one side, and Rome on the other, and that we might combine the ceremonialism and sacramentalism of St. Peter's on the Tiber with the freedom from corruption and ecclesiastical independence of St. Paul's on the Thames.

He did not, in short, want to go back to the Vatican, but he wanted to borrow some of its principles, and plant them in Lambeth Palace. I see in these ideas and theories a key to all his policy. His one aim from St. John's, Oxford 'till he was sent to the Tower, was not to Romanize, but to un-Protestantize the Church of England. Some may think this a nice and too refined a distinction. I do not. A "Romanizer" is one thing, an "un-Protestantizer" is another.

This was the explanation of his always opposing what he called "Calvinism." He would fain have made popular Protestant theology odious by painting the doctrines of grace as inseparable from antinomianism and extreme views of election and reprobation. He knew too well that nothing so damages a theological cause as a cleverly chosen nickname.

This was the explanation of his making so much ado about the position of the Lord's Table. It was not merely to preserve the Table from irreverent and profane uses, but to exalt the sacrament of the Lord's Supper, and make a slight approach to the sacrifice of the Mass.

This was the explanation of his advocating extravagant views of the Episcopal office, as if it were essential to a Church. It helped his favourite notion that the Church of England occupied a middle position between the Presbyterian Church of Geneva and the Church of Rome—an idea, by the way, often brought forward nowadays, and about as absurd as to say the Isle of Wight occupies a middle position between England and France!

This was the explanation of his incessantly persecuting and teasing lecturers, and discouraging doctrinal preaching all over the land. He wished to make people think that the sacraments, and not the preaching of God's Word, were the principal part of Christianity.

This was the explanation of his introducing, as far as possible, such histrionic ceremonials as those with which he astonished London at the consecration of St. Catherine Cree. He desired to show the public that Churchmen could have as much sensuous and showy religion as Papists; and that, if we did not have the Mass itself, the Communion Service of the Prayer Book might be so managed and manipulated as to make an excellent imitation of it.

This was the explanation of his discouraging and checking all attacks on Popery, whether in the pulpit or the press, and obliging whole passages in many good books of the time to be expurgated and suppressed. He wished to lower the tone of the country about the nature of Popery, and to make people less alive to its enormous evils and less awake to his own movements.

This, in the last place, but not least, was the explanation of his constantly promoting and bringing forward in the Church Arminian and semi-Protestant divines of his own school of theology. Wren, Montague, and Mainwaring are specimens of the kind of men he delighted to honour. He never threw away an opportunity of this kind. He knew the importance of backing your friends, and of securing all the good things of place, power, and influence for your own party. One plan was always kept in view, and that was to fill up the Bench, as far as possible, with High Churchmen.

Such, I believe firmly, is the true account of Laud's policy. He had always one aim before him. Of that aim he never lost sight for a day. And while we admire his consistency, his persistency, his dogged tenacity of purpose, we must never forget the real nature of his aim. It was to un-Protestantize the Church of England.

The consequences of Laud's policy

One more question demands a few words. What were the consequences of Laud's policy? I shall say but little on this point. Some people, I believe, who regard him as a slandered person, and venerate him as the reviver of so-called Catholic principles, would tell you that he did a great deal of good. From such I take leave to differ entirely. I hold that he did more harm to the Reformed Church of England than any man that ever lived—more than Gardiner, Bonner, Cardinal Pole, and Bloody Mary, all put together. I have already said that he probably meant well, and acted conscientiously. I quite believe that he thought his policy was doing God and the Church of England good service. But the consequences of his policy, both direct and indirect, were disastrous, mischievous, and evil in the extreme. Let me show you what they were.

One direct consequence of Laud's policy was a widespread decline of sound Protestant feeling among the clergy, from which our Church has never recovered. The principles and opinions of a forward, pushing Archbishop like him, who practically had the key of all patronage in his pocket, were only too greedily swallowed by many. A school of divines was rapidly gathered and consolidated within our pale which has weakened our Church most seriously from that period. How deep and widespread this decline was may be gathered from the *Memoirs of Panzani*, the Romish emissary to England in Laud's days, where he gives an account of the state of things in this country. He particularly mentions that Laud's great friend, Bishop Montague, told him privately, in 1636, that "he and many of his brethren were prepared to conform themselves to the method and discipline of the Gallican Church;" and, "that there were only three Bishops on the bench that could be counted violently bent against the Church of Rome: viz., Morton, Davenant, and Hall;" and, "as for the aversion to Popery which we discover in our sermons and printed books," said Montague, "they are things of form, chiefly to humour the populace and not to be much regarded." Pretty language this from an English Bishop! But what an idea it gives us of the rapid spread of Laud's theology!

But another direct consequence of Laud's policy was of a very different kind. There arose throughout the land a spirit of thorough alienation of the middle classes from the Church of England. The mass of English people gradually began to dislike a religious body which they saw principally occupied in persecuting Puritanism, silencing preachers, checking zeal, exalting forms, deifying sacraments, and complimenting Popery. The multitude seldom draws nice distinctions. It measures institutions chiefly by their working and administration, and cares little for theories and great principles. Little by little men's minds throughout the country began to connect episcopacy with tyranny, the liturgy with formality, and the Church of England with fines, imprisonments, and punishments.

Baxter's autobiography gives a vivid picture of the universal feeling of the kind which prevailed. Hence, when the Long Parliament assembled, there was a most painful unanimity of ill-feeling towards the poor old Church of England. The members representing all the counties and boroughs in England, with few exceptions, were found thoroughly dissatisfied with the Establishment; and the assailants, both in number and influence, completely swamped and overwhelmed the defenders. And all this was the doing of Laud! He had disgusted the bulk of the laity, lost the middle classes, and turned the Church's friends into foes.

The last and worst direct consequence of Laud's policy was the temporary destruction of the Church of England. An ecclesiastical revolution took place, which swelled at length into a kind of reign of terror. The pent-up feelings of the middle classes, once let loose, broke out into a hurricane, before which everything in the framework of the Church of England was clean swept away. Bishops, and deans, and clergy, and Liturgy, were all shovelled off the stage like so much rubbish. Good things as well as bad were involved in one common ruin. A bloody civil war broke out. Charles I followed Strafford and Laud to the scaffold. Everything in Church and State was turned upside down. Order at last was only kept by the iron hand of a military dictator, Oliver Cromwell. The crown and the mitre were both alike proscribed, excommunicated, and rolled in the dust. And all this was the doing of Laud! He sowed the wind and reaped the whirlwind.

Such were the direct consequences of Laud's policy. I wish they had been all the harm that he did. But, unhappily, there were other indirect consequences, of which we feel the bad effects to this very day. The whole balance of English feeling about the Church of England was completely disarranged and disturbed by his proceedings. Equilibrium has never been recovered.

A pendulum was set swinging by his mischievous folly, which has now oscillated violently for 200 years. First came a strong reaction in favour of the Church when the Stuarts returned to the throne at the Restoration, having learned nothing and forgotten nothing. Moderation and tolerance, you will remember, were then thrown to the winds. The wretched Act of Uniformity was passed, by which 2,000 of the best clergy of the age were turned out of our pale, and lost to our ranks for ever.

Then came a long and dreary time of exhaustion and stagnation, a time during which the Church of England, like a torpid sloth, existed indeed, and hung on the State tree, but scarcely lived, moved, or breathed.

Then came, after a century, the revival of true Protestant religion under the auspices of those glorious clergymen Wesley and Whitefield; but a revival which our Bishops could neither understand, appreciate, direct, manage, utilise, encourage, or retain. Then came the permanent establishment of Methodism and a vast increase of nonconformity.

Finally, we see in our own days the spectacle of a pure Protestant Church in England which has allowed half the population to stray out of its fold and slip out of its fingers, and is neither liked, nor trusted, nor valued by the great majority of dissentients! And what was the first cause of all this? I answer again, in one sentence, the fatal policy of Archbishop Laud! He sowed the seed of which we reap the consequences. He made a whole generation of Englishmen hate the Church of England and feel no confidence in her; and the feeling survives and lingers down to the present day.

Lessons for today

It only remains for me now to point out the leading lessons which Laud's history ought to teach us. I have done my best to show you the man, and his character, and his policy, and the consequences of it. On each of these topics, you will readily believe, much more might be said. But I am obliged to skim the surface of things, and leave much to be filled up by my readers. If I can only set men thinking and reading, and send them to such books as Marsden's *History of the Puritans*, and Stoughton's *Ecclesiastical History*, I shall, even in this short sketch, have not laboured in vain. Let me now try to make some practical use of the whole subject.

It is dangerous to un-Protestantize the Church of England

The first lesson that I draw from the subject is this. Laud's history shows us, that any attempt to un-Protestantize the Church of England is fraught with peril and mischief to the Establishment. Any man—no matter how high his rank—Archbishop, Bishop, Dean, or Archdeacon; no matter how high his character— earnest, zealous, conscientious, learned, devout, charitable, and self-denying;—any man who tries to reintroduce Romish doctrines and Romish ceremonies into the Church of England, is an enemy to the Establishment, and is damaging its best interests.

I am no more infallible than the Pope. I have no access to peculiar information more than other men. But it is my firm and decided conviction, that the bulk of Churchmen in our days will not have Romanism brought back within our pale. Some, perhaps, of the aristocracy and the nobility may approve a sensuous, histrionic religion, and see no harm in a nearer approximation to the ways of Rome. But the majority of the middle classes, and the most intelligent of the lower orders, will not have Romanism in any shape, or at any price; and if you try to thrust it down their throats, they will just leave the Church to shift for itself, and walk away. There will be no more reign of terror, or ecclesiastical earthquakes. There will be no repetition of State trials. The Lauds and Montagues on our bench, if any, will not be taken to Tower Hill and beheaded. But the middle classes will just leave bishops, deans, and clergy alone in their glory, and forsake the Establishment. The cry will be raised, "This is not our rest, for it is polluted with Romanism: we must depart hence. To your tents, O Israel!"

And what will happen then? Why, the Church will perish for want of Churchmen. Generals, and colonels, and band, alone, do not make up an army; and bishops, and deans, and choristers, and clergy, alone, do not make up a Church. Disestablishment will come as a matter of course. The Church of a minority will not be long spared on this side of St. George's Channel any more than on the other. The tender mercies of liberal statesmen may perhaps leave the poor old Church, her cathedrals, and parish churches, and possibly some part of her endowments. But if the "multitude of people" is the glory of a church as well as of a prince, the glory of the Church of England will have passed away for ever. "Ichabod" will be written over empty naves and choirs. The Establishment will split up, or become one of the sects, like the Scotch Episcopal Church, and the page of history will record that she made shipwreck of all her greatness by the suicidal attempt to recede from Protestantism and reintroduce Popery.

No! If I know anything of the middle classes and intelligent lower orders, they wish to have a Protestant Establishment, or no Establishment at all. They may not be hard readers or deep thinkers. But they know what Romanism was 350 years ago, and they do not want it back. They know what priestly tyranny, and the sacrifice of the Mass, and the odious confessional, did before the Reformation. They have an innate, instinctive, wholesome dislike of the slightest symptom of any return to these things. They cannot draw nice distinctions; they are apt to call a spade a spade, and to give things their right names. And if they see any attempt to imitate Romanism in our churches, and to counterfeit Romish ceremonies, their suspicions are roused at once. The clergyman who rouses these suspicions, I say boldly, however earnest, conscientious, well-meaning, and charitable, is no friend to the Church of England, and is doing immense harm.

Harm may be done to a Church by a very small party

The second lesson of the subject is this. Laud's history shows us what harm may be done to a Church by a very small party. Great is the power of a minority when it acts together, and is united. Great is the influence of a few determined men when they combine for mischief, see their object clearly, and endeavour incessantly and unscrupulously to carry it out. Laud's beginnings at St. John's, Oxford were very small, but his latter end greatly increased.

This is a point, I venture to say, which is far too much overlooked. Nothing has injured the Church of England so much in the last thirty years as the habit of underrating and despising the Tractarian movement. How small it seemed, when it first began under Newman, Pusey, Keble, and Richard Froude. It was a cloud which looked no bigger than a man's hand! To what portentous proportions, comparatively, it has now grown. A black thunderstorm seems to overspread one half the heavens.

Well do I remember a valued Oxford friend, now dead, calling the attention of Bishop Sumner (of Chester) and Chancellor Raikes to this subject, fifty years ago, in a private conversation. Well do I remember the quiet smile of incredulity with which those venerable men listened, evidently thinking us young, short-sighted alarmists. "It was but a temporary delusion; it would soon pass away." *Nubecula est; transibit.*[29] I thought, then, that they did not rightly estimate the extent of the danger. I suspect they both lived to change their minds.

Let us, then, not underrate the power of Ritualism because its adherents seem a small party, and the churches where they play at Popery are comparatively few in number. The party is not so small as it appears. It has many sympathisers throughout the country, who only wait for the time when they can show their colours, and at the first shift of wind will put to sea. It must not be despised because it is small. Minorities often prove winners in the long run.

No! We ought to remember the great Duke of Wellington's maxim, that it is a cardinal mistake in war, and a cause of great disasters, to undervalue your enemy. We must make up our mind that the Ritualistic movement of this day is a very serious affair, and that it requires the utmost exertions of sound Churchmen to prevent it ruining the Church of England. When we can afford to despise a little spark in a powder magazine, a little crack in a sea-wall embankment, a little leak in a ship, a little flaw in a chain cable, a few traitors in the garrison of a citadel, then, and not till then, it will be time to pooh-pooh Ritualism, because its avowed adherents, like Laud's party at first, seem at present comparatively few.

The Laity must take an interest in the condition of the Church

The last lesson I draw from our subject is this. Laud's history shows us the immense importance of the laity taking timely interest in the condition of the Church of England. Nothing, it is clear to me, preserved the Church of England from returning bodily to Popery, two hundred years ago, but the active interference of the laity. I do not say it would have happened in Laud's time. I do not think he ever meant the Pope at

---

[29] "It's only a little cloud; it will pass." An ironic use of Athanasius' comment about Arian persecution—*Editor*.

Lambeth to be subject to the Pope at the Vatican. But I do believe that another twenty years of unopposed, systematic, persistent un-Protestantizing would have "educated" a generation of semi-Papists, and paved the way for downright Popery. From this we were not preserved by the bishops and clergy, but by the laity taking up the matter in the House of Commons.

I grant their remedies were violent, and their surgery coarse and savage. They let blood profusely, and did great harm in some directions, if they did good in others. But one thing I always maintain was done by Hollis, Dering, Pym, Hampden, and their companions. They prevented the nation going back to Babylon. They stamped out Popery for the time in the Church of England. Even the civil war was better than the return of Popery. Pent and torn by conflicting parties, her very existence is in peril. Never was there a Church which had within her pale such totally opposite schools of theology. This state of things cannot last. The question may well rise in many minds, "What shall be the end? We cannot go on as we are. Will the sick man live, or will he die?"

I hope the laity of this day will never forget this. They are the real hope of the Church of England. Our future depends greatly on their conduct and line of action. If they sit still and let things take their own course, I see nothing but evil before us. If they arise in their might, like their forefathers, and demand that there shall be no Romish innovations, no un-Protestantizing practices allowed in our communion, there is yet ground for hope. It is not too late to win a battle. Once let the laity raise the old cry,—"*Nolumus leges Angliæ mutari!*"[30] We will have a Protestant Establishment or none at all!"—and I shall not despair of the Church of England.

One thing, in conclusion, is very clear. Whatever we may think about Laud, the Church of England is in a very critical position. Every one who reflects must confess this. Her rowers have brought her into troubled waters. Rent and torn by conflicting parties, her very existence is in peril.

---

30 "We do not want the laws of England to change!" An ironic use of Charles I's words to Parliament!—*Editor.*

Never was there a Church which had within her pale such totally opposite schools of theology. This state of things cannot last. The question may well rise in many minds, "What shall be the end? We cannot go on as we are. Will the sick man live, or will he die?"

As usual in such cases, advice is plentiful, the doctors are many, and the prescriptions abound—some homœopathic and some allopathic. Every one has his "panacea" and his "Eirenicon." "Only use it," he cries, "and the Church will be cured." Wider terms of communion, relaxation of creeds and articles, liturgical revision, synodical action, increase of the Episcopate, union of the Western Churches —all these are remedies gravely propounded and earnestly thrust on our attention. Each has its advocates, and each is warranted to cure. I have not the slightest faith in any of these healing measures. Two or three of them are downright mischievous. The best of them is not the medicine for the time. I regard them all as utterly beside the mark, and unable to touch the disease.

My own mind is thoroughly made up. I know of only one cure and remedy for the ailments of our beloved Church. That remedy is a revival among us of thorough Protestant principles and Protestant theology—the principles of the glorious Reformation, the theology of Latimer, and Hooper, and Jewel. Whether God will grant us such a revival I cannot tell: perhaps our days are numbered. Without such a revival I have little hope for the future. We shall only fall lower and lower, and at last our candlestick will be removed, like that of Ephesus. Give us such a revival, and I hope everything. The laity would rally round us once more—the Spirit of God would be poured on our congregations. God, even the Lord God of our fathers, would give us his blessing.

I said the laity would rally round us. I say it advisedly. At present a large number of the best of them ride at single anchor, and hold by the Church of England with a very loose hand. They are tired, wearied, and disgusted with the undisturbed growth and progress of semi-Popery. They see no use in Protestant Bishops and Articles, if Romanism is allowed to sit in the house of God. They may not be deep theologians, or very conversant with Catholic principles and primitive antiquity. But they are not hard to satisfy. They know and feel what does them good. They want plain Protestant worship, and plain Protestant preaching, and if they cannot have these in the Establishment they will soon migrate and swarm off elsewhere. The bulk of our middle classes and educated lower orders in the Church do not want chasubles, copes, dalmatics, birettas, banners, processions, incense, pastoral staffs, crucifixes, incessant bowings, turnings, and genuflections, or any such pernicious trumpery. Such things are mere gaudy toys, which may please children, and satisfy idle young men and women, and the whole herd of the ignorant, the weak-minded, and the superstitious. But they do not meet the wants of the middle-aged, the hard-headed, the hard-working men and women of the middle and lower orders. They want food—food for heart, and food for conscience; and if they do not find it in the Established Church of England, they will walk off and seek it elsewhere. Give them plain, simple, hearty Bible worship—plain, simple, hearty Bible preaching. Give them the old, old story of Christ upon the cross, the real work of the Holy Ghost felt and experienced in the inner man. Give them the noble lessons of repentance, faith, holiness. Give them these, and they will never forsake the Church of England.[31]

I repeat it emphatically. A return to downright Protestant principles and Protestant theology is the Church's want in the present day. It is the only medicine which will heal the Church's disease.

I now wind up my paper with a short passage from the pen of a great man, which deserves special attention, partly because of his name and character, and partly because he wrote it with death before his eyes. The man I speak of is Lord William Russell, who was beheaded in Lincoln's Inn Fields on a false charge of treason, in the reign of Charles the Second, 1683. The book I find it in is *The Life of Lord W. Russell*, written by the late Earl Russell in 1820. The paper in which the passage occurs was

---

31 *The Times* of March 29th 1869 says most truly, "Ritualistic services may attract curious or admiring crowds, but they neither bring the poor to church nor bring religion into the homes of the poor."

given by the noble sufferer to his friends only a few moments before his execution. He says:—

> I did believe, and do still believe, that Popery is breaking in upon this nation, and that those who advance it will stop at nothing to carry on their designs. ... I am heartily sorry that so many Protestants give their helping hand to it. But I hope God will preserve the Protestant religion and this nation, though I am afraid it will pass under very great trials and very great sufferings.

Solemn words these, and painfully prophetic! Well would it be for this country, in the nineteenth century, if English Peers and English Prelates, English Members of Parliament and English Clergymen, saw the danger of Popery "breaking in upon this nation" as clearly as did, in the seventeenth century, the dying patriot, Lord W. Russell.

Note

The following extracts from Mr. Hallam's *Constitutional History of England* appear to me to deserve particular attention. I think so, because they contain the deliberate opinion of a well-read layman, of no extreme theological views, and of one who has justly obtained a world-wide reputation on account of his learning, his correct judgment, and his impartiality:

> Laud's talents, though enabling him to acquire a large portion of theological learning, seem to have been by no means considerable. There cannot be a more contemptible work than this Diary; and his letters to Strafford display some smartness, but no great capacity. He managed, indeed, his own defence when impeached with some ability; but on such occasions ordinary men are apt to put forth a remarkable readiness and ability. . . . Though not literally destitute of religion, it was so subordinate to worldly interest, and so blended in his mind with the impure alloy of temporal pride, that he became an intolerant persecutor of the Puritan clergy, not from bigotry, which in its usual sense he never displayed, but systematic policy. And being subject, as his friends call it, to some infirmities of temper—that is, choleric,

vindictive, harsh, and even cruel to a great degree—he not only took a prominent share in the severities of the Star Chamber, but perpetually lamented that he was restrained from going further lengths.[32]

All the innovations of the school of Laud were so many approaches in the exterior worship of the Church to the Roman model. Pictures were set up or repaired; the Communion Table took the name of an altar; it was sometimes made of stone; obeisances were made to it; the crucifix was sometimes placed upon it; the dress of the officiating priests became more gaudy; churches were consecrated with strange and mystical pageantry. These petty superstitions, which would of themselves have disgusted a nation accustomed to despise as well as abhor the pompous rites of the Catholics, became more alarming from the evident bias of some leading Churchmen to parts of the Romish theology. The doctrine of a real presence, distinguishable only by vagueness of definition from that of the Church of Rome, was generally held. Montague, Bishop of Chichester, already conspicuous and justly reckoned the chief of the Romanizing faction, went a considerable length towards admitting the invocation of saints. Prayers for the dead, which lead at once to the tenet of purgatory, were vindicated by many. In fact, there was hardly any distinctive opinion of the Church of Rome which had not its abettors among the Bishops, or those who wrote under their patronage.[33]

---

32 Hallam's *Constitutional History of England*, Volume 2, page 54.

33 *Ibid.*, page 86 (1832 edition).

3. Samuel Ward

Samuel Ward, an eminent Suffolk divine, and one of the most famous Puritans of the seventeenth century, is a man whose name is comparatively unknown to most readers of English theology. This is easily accounted for. He wrote but little, and what he wrote has never been reprinted till very lately. The works of Owen, Baxter, Gurnal, Charnock, Goodwin, Adams, Brooks, Watson, Greenhill, Sibbes, Jenkyn, Manton, Burroughs, Bolton, and others, have been reprinted, either wholly or partially. Of Samuel Ward, so far as I can ascertain, not a word had been reprinted till recently for more than two hundred years.

How far Samuel Ward's sermons have deserved this neglect, I am content to leave to the judgment of all students of theology into whose hands his sermons may fall. But I venture the opinion, that it reflects little credit on the discretion of republishers of old divinity that such a writer as Samuel Ward has been so long passed over. His case, however, does not stand alone. When such works as those of Swinnock, Arrowsmith on John 1, Gouge on Hebrews, Airay on Philippians, John Rogers on 1 Peter, Hardy on 1 John, Daniel Rogers on Naaman the Syrian (to say nothing of some of the best works of Manton and Brooks), have been only recently thought worthy of republication, we must not be surprised at the treatment which Ward has received.

As one who was for thirty-seven years a Suffolk minister, and a thorough lover of Puritan theology, I desire to supply some information about

Ward in this biographical paper. I should have been especially pleased if it had been in my power to write a complete memoir of the man and his ministry. I regret, however, to be obliged to say that the materials from which any account of him can be compiled are exceedingly scanty, and the facts known about him are comparatively few. Nor yet, unhappily, is this difficulty the only one with which I have had to contend. It is a very curious circumstance, that no less than three divines named "S. Ward" lived in the first half of the seventeenth century, and were all members of Sidney College, Cambridge. These three were Dr. Samuel Ward, Master of Sidney College, who was one of the English Commissioners at the Synod of Dort, and a correspondent of Archbishop Usher; Seth Ward, who was successively Bishop of Exeter and Salisbury; and Samuel Ward, of Ipswich, whose sermons have been lately reprinted.

Of these three, the two "Samuels" were undoubtedly the most remarkable men; but the similarity of their names has hitherto involved their biographies in much confusion. I can only say that I have done my best, in the face of these accumulated difficulties, to unravel a tangled skein, and to supply the reader with accurate information.

The Life of Samuel Ward

The story of Samuel Ward's life is soon told. He was born at Haverhill, in Suffolk, in the year 1577, and was eldest son of the Rev. John Ward, Minister of the Gospel in that town. John Ward, the father of Samuel Ward, appears to have been a man of considerable eminence as a minister and preacher. Fuller (in his *Worthies of Suffolk*) says that the three sons together would not make up the abilities of their father. The following inscription on his tomb in Haverhill Church is well worth reading:—

Johannes Warde.

Quo si quis scivit scitius,
Aut si quis docuit doctius,
At rarus vixit sanctius,
Et nullus tonuit fortius.[34]

Son of thunder, son of ye dove,
Full of hot zeal, full of true love;
In preaching truth, in living right,
A burning lampe, a shining light.

Light Here.   **Stars Hereafter.**

Watch. John Ward, after he with great evidence and power of ye Spirite, and with much fruit, preached ye Gospel at Haverill and Bury in Suff. 25 years, was heere gathered to his fathers. Susan, his widdowe, married Rogers, that worthy Pastor of Wethersfielde. He left 3 sonnes, Samuel, Nathaniel, John, Preachers, who for them and theirs, wish no greater blessing than that they may continue in beleeving and preaching the same Gospel till ye coming of Christ. Come, Lord Jesus, come quicklye. **Warde.**

Watch. Death is our entrance into life. **Warde.**

Samuel Ward, the subject of this memoir was admitted a scholar of St. John's College, Cambridge on Lady Margaret's foundation, on Lord Burghley's nomination, November 6th, 1594, and went out B.A. of that house in 1596. He was appointed one of the first Fellows of Sidney Sussex College in 1599, commenced M.A. 1600, vacated his Fellowship on his marriage in 1604, and proceeded B.D. in 1607.

---

34 This could be translated:
Of knowledge, some may have greater store, While some are more learned in teaching;
But rarely was there holiness more, And never such thunder in preaching.—*Editor*.

Nothing is known of Ward's boyhood and youth. His entrance on the work of the ministry, the name of the Bishop by whom he was ordained, the date of his ordination, the place where he first began to do Christ's work as a preacher, are all things of which apparently there is no record. His first appearance as a public character was in the capacity of Lecturer at his native town of Haverhill. Of his success at Haverhill, Samuel Clark, in his *Lives of Eminent Persons* (page 154 in the 1683 edition), gives the following interesting example, in his life of Samuel Fairclough, a famous minister of Kedington, in Suffolk:

> God was pleased to begin a work of grace in the heart of Samuel Fairclough very early and betimes, by awakening his conscience by the terror of the law, and by bestowing a sincere repentance upon him thereby, and by working an effectual faith in him; and all this was done by the ministry of the Word preached by Mr. Samuel Ward, then Lecturer of Haverhill. Mr. Ward had answered for him in baptism, and had always a hearty love to him.
>
> Preaching one day on the conversion of Zaccheus, and discoursing upon his fourfold restitution in cases of rapine and extortion, Mr. Ward used that frequent expression, that no man can expect pardon from God of the wrong done to another's estate, except he make full restitution to the wronged person, if it may possibly be done. This was as a dart directed by the hand of God to the heart of young Fairclough, who, together with one John Trigg, afterwards a famous physician in London, had the very week before robbed the orchard of one Goodman Jude of that town, and had filled their pockets as well as their bellies with the fruit of a mellow pear tree.
>
> At and after sermon, young Fairclough mourned much and had not any sleep all the night following; and, rising on the Monday morning, he went to his companion Trigg and told him that he was going to Goodman Jude's, to carry him twelve pence by way of restitution for three pennyworth of pears of which he had wronged him. Trigg, fearing that if the thing were confessed to Jude, he would acquaint

Robotham their master therewith, and that corporal correction would follow, did earnestly strive to divert the poor child from his purpose of restitution. But Fairclough replied that God would not pardon the sin except restitution were made. To which Trigg answered thus: 'Thou talkest like a fool, Sam; God will forgive us ten times sooner than old Jude will forgive us once.'

But our Samuel was of another mind, and therefore he goes on to Jude's house, and there told him his errand, and offered him a shilling, which Jude refusing (though he declared his forgiveness of the wrong), the youth's wound smarted so, that he could get no rest till he went to his spiritual father, Mr. Ward, and opened to him the whole state of his soul, both on account of this particular sin and many others, and most especially the sin of sins, the original sin and depravation of his nature. Mr. Ward received him with great affection and tenderness, and proved the good Samaritan to him, pouring wine and oil into his wounds, answering all his questions, satisfying his fears, and preaching Jesus to him so fully and effectually that he became a true and sincere convert, and dedicated and devoted himself to his Saviour and Redeemer all the days of his life after.[35]

From Haverhill, Samuel Ward was removed in 1603 at the early age of twenty-six, to a position of great importance in those days. He was appointed by the Corporation of Ipswich to the office of Town Preacher at Ipswich, and filled the pulpit of St. Mary-le-Tower in that town with little intermission for about thirty years. Ipswich and Norwich, it must be remembered, were places of far more importance two hundred and fifty years ago than they are at the present day. They were the capital towns of two of the wealthiest and most thickly peopled counties in England. Suf-

---

35 I think it right to remark that Clark, in all probability, has erred in his dates in telling this story. He says that Fairclough was born in 1594, and that the event he has recorded took place when he was thirteen years old. Now, in 1607 Ward had ceased to be Lecturer of Haverhill. Whether the explanation of this discrepancy is that Fairclough was born before 1594, or that he was only nine years old when he stole the pears, or that Ward was visiting at Haverhill in 1607 and preached during his visit, or that Fairclough was at school at Ipswich and not Haverhill, is a point that we have no means of deciding.

folk, in particular, was a county in which the Protestant and Evangelical principles of the Reformation had taken particularly deep root. Some of the most eminent Puritans were Suffolk ministers. To be chosen Town Preacher of a place like Ipswich two hundred and fifty years ago was a very great honour, and shows the high estimate which was set on Samuel Ward's ministerial character, even when he was so young as twenty-six. It deserves to be remarked that Matthew Lawrence and Stephen Marshall, who were among his successors, were both leading men among the divines of the seventeenth century.

The influence which Ward possessed in Ipswich appears to have been very considerable. Fuller says, "He was preferred Minister *in*, or rather *of*, Ipswich, having a care over, and a love from, all the parishes in that populous place. Indeed, he had a magnetic virtue (as if he had learned it from the loadstone, in whose qualities he was so knowing) to attract people's affections."[36]

The history of his thirty years' ministry in the town of Ipswich would doubtless prove full of interesting particulars, if we could only discover them. Unhappily, I can only supply the reader with the following dry facts, which I have found in an antiquarian publication of considerable value, entitled *Wodderspoon's Memorials of Ipswich*. They are evidently compiled from ancient records, and throw some useful light on certain points of Ward's history.

Wodderspoon says,—

> In the year 1603, on All Saints' Day, a man of considerable eminence was elected as Preacher, Mr. Samuel Ward. The Corporation appear to have treated him with great liberality, appointing an hundred marks as his stipend, and also allowing him £6 13s. 4d. quarterly in addition, for house rent.

---

36 I suspect that Fuller's remarks about the loadstone refer to a book called *Magnetis Reductorium Theologium*, which is sometimes attributed to Samuel Ward of Ipswich. But it is more than doubtful whether the authorship of this book does not belong to Dr. Samuel Ward, the Principal of Sidney College, of whom mention has already been made.

The Municipal Authorities (possibly because of obtaining so able a divine) declare very minutely the terms of Mr. Ward's engagement. In his sickness or absence he is to provide for the supply of a minister at the usual place three times a week, 'as usual hath been.' 'He shall not be absent out of town above forty days in one year, without leave; and if he shall take a pastoral charge, his retainer by the Corporation is to be void. The pension granted to him is not to be charged on the Foundation or Hospital Lands.'

In the seventh year of James I, the Corporation purchased a house for the Preacher, or rather for Mr. Ward. This house was bought by the town contributing £120, and the rest of the money was made up by free contributions, on the understanding that, when Mr. Ward ceased to be Preacher, the building was to be re-sold, and the various sums collected returned to those who contributed, as well as the money advanced by the Corporation.

In the eighth year of James I, the Corporation increased the salary of Mr. Ward to £90 per annum,' on account of the charges he is at by abiding here.'

In the fourteenth year of James I, Mr. Samuel Ward's pension increased from £90 to £100 yearly.

The preaching of this divine, being of so free and puritanic a character, did not long escape the notice of the tale-bearers of the Court; and after a short period, spent in negotiation, Mr. Ward was restrained from officiating in his office. In 1623, August 6th, a record appears in the town books, to the effect that 'a letter from the King, to inhibit Mr. Ward from preaching, is referred to the Council of the town.

About the remaining portion of Ward's life, Wodderspoon supplies no information. The little that we know about it is gleaned from other sources.

It is clear, from Hackett's life of the Lord Keeper Bishop Williams (page 95 of the 1603 edition), that though prosecuted by Bishop Harsnet for nonconformity in 1623, Ward was only suspended temporarily, if at all, from his office as Preacher. Brook in his *Lives of the Puritans* (Volume 2, page 452), following Hackett, says, that "upon his prosecution in the Consistory of Norwich, he appealed from the Bishop to the King, who committed the articles exhibited against him to the examination of the Lord Keeper Williams." The Lord Keeper reported that Mr. Ward "was not altogether blameless, but a man easily to be won by fair dealing; and persuaded Bishop Harsnet to take his submission, and not remove him from Ipswich. The truth is, the Lord Keeper found that Mr. Ward possessed so much candour, and was so ready to promote the interests of the Church, that he could do no less than compound the troubles of so learned and industrious a divine. He was therefore released from the prosecution, and most probably continued for some time without molestation in the peaceable exercise of his ministry." Brook might here have added a fact, recorded by Hackett, that Ward was so good a friend to the Church of England that he was the means of retaining several persons who were wavering about conformity, within the pale of the Episcopal communion.

After eleven years of comparative quiet, Ward was prosecuted again for alleged nonconformity, at the instigation of Archbishop Laud. Prynne, in his account of Laud's trial (page 361), tells us that in the year 1635, he was impeached in the High Commission Court for preaching against bowing at the name of Jesus, and against the Book of Sports, and for having said "that the Church of England was ready to ring changes in religion," and "that the gospel stood on tiptoe ready to be gone." He was found guilty, was enjoined to make a public recantation in such form as the Court should appoint, and condemned in costs of the suit. Upon his refusal to recant, he was committed to prison, where he remained a long time.

In a note to Brook's account of this disgraceful transaction, which he appears to have gathered out of Rushworth's *Collections* and Wharton's *Troubles of Laud*, he mentions a remarkable fact about Ward at this juncture of his life, which shows the high esteem in which he was held at Ipswich. It appears that after his suspension the Bishop of Norwich would have allowed his people another minister in his place; but "they would have Mr. Ward, or none!"

The last four years of Ward's life are a subject on which I find it very difficult to discover the truth. Brook says that after his release from prison he retired to Holland, and became a colleague of William Bridge, the famous Independent minister of Yarmouth, who had settled at Rotterdam. He also mentions a report that he and Mr. Bridge renounced their Episcopal ordination, and were re-ordained: "Mr. Bridge ordaining Mr. Ward, and Mr. Ward returning the compliment." He adds another report that Ward was unjustly deposed from his pastoral office at Rotterdam, and after a short interval restored.

I venture to think that this account must be regarded with some suspicion. At any rate, I doubt whether we are in possession of all the facts in the transaction which Brook records. That Ward retired to Holland after his release from prison is highly probable. It was a step which many were constrained to take for the sake of peace and liberty of conscience in the days of the Stuarts. That he was pastor of a Church at Rotterdam, in conjunction with Bridge, that differences arose between him and his colleague, that he was temporarily deposed from his office and afterward restored, are things which I think very likely.

His re-ordination is a point which I think questionable. For one thing, it seems to me exceedingly improbable that a man of Ward's age and standing would first be re-ordained by Bridge, who was twenty-three years younger than himself, and afterward re-ordain Bridge. For another thing, it appears very strange that a man who had renounced his Episcopal orders, should have afterwards received an honourable burial in the aisle of an Ipswich church, in the year 1639.

One thing only is clear. Ward's stay at Rotterdam could not have been very lengthy. He was not committed to prison till 1635 and was buried in 1639. He "lay in prison long," according to Prynne. At any rate, he lay there long enough to write a Latin work, called, *A Rapture*, of which it is expressly stated that it was composed during his imprisonment "in the Gate House." In 1638 we find him buying a house in Ipswich. It is plain at this rate that he could not have been very long in Holland.

However, the whole of the transactions at Rotterdam, so far as Ward is concerned, are involved in some obscurity. Stories against eminent Puritans were easily fabricated and greedily swallowed in the seventeenth century. Brook's assertion that Ward died in Holland, about 1640, is so entirely destitute of foundation, that it rather damages the value of his account of Ward's latter days.

Granting, however, that after his release from prison Ward retired to Holland, there seems every reason to believe that he returned to Ipswich early in 1638. It appears from the town books of Ipswich (according to Wodderspoon), that in April, 1638, he purchased the house provided for him by the town for £140, repaying the contributors the sum contributed by them. He died in the month of March, 1639, aged 62; and was buried in St. Mary-le-Tower, Ipswich, on the 8th of that month. A certified copy of the entry of his burial, in the parish register, is in my possession. On a stone which was laid in his lifetime in the middle aisle of the church, the following words (according to Clarke's *History of Ipswich*) are still extant:—

> "Watch, Ward! yet a little while,
> And He that shall come, will come."

Under this stone it is supposed the bones of the good old Puritan preacher were laid; and to this day he is spoken of by those who know his name in Ipswich as "Watch Ward."

It only remains to add, that Ward married, in 1604, a widow named Deborah Bolton, of Isleham in Cambridge, and had by her a family.[37]

It is an interesting fact, recorded in the town books of Ipswich, that after his death, as a mark of respect, his widow and his eldest son Samuel were allowed for their lives the stipend enjoyed by their father: viz., £100 annually. It is also worthy of remark, that he had two brothers who were ministers, John and Nathaniel. John Ward lived and died Rector of St. Clement's, Ipswich and there is a tablet and short inscription about him

---

37 For this fact, and the facts about Ward's degrees at Cambridge, I am indebted to a well-informed writer in *Notes and Queries* for October, 1861.

in that church. Nathaniel Ward was Minister of Standon, Herts., went to America in 1634, returned to England in 1646, and died at Shenfield in Essex, 1653.

There is an excellent portrait of Ward still extant in Ipswich. He is represented with an open book in his right hand, a ruff round his neck, a peaked beard and moustaches. On one side is a coast beacon lighted; and there is an inscription:

"Watche Ward. Ætatis suæ, 43. 1620."

The following extract, from a rare volume called *The Tombstone; or, a notice and imperfect monument of that worthy man, Mr. John Carter, Pastor of Bramford and Belstead, in Suffolk* (1653), will probably be thought to deserve insertion, as an incidental evidence of the high esteem in which Ward was held in the neighbourhood of Ipswich. The work was written by Mr. Carter's son and the extract describes what occurred at his father's funeral. He says (at pages 26-27),

> In the afternoon, February 4th 1634, at my father's interring, there was a great confluence of people from all parts thereabout, ministers, and others taking up the word of Joash, King of Israel, 'O my father! my father! the chariots of Israel and the horsemen thereof!' Old Mr. Samuel Ward, that famous divine, and the glory of Ipswich, came to the funeral, brought a mourning gown with him, and offered very respectfully to preach the funeral sermon, seeing that such a congregation was gathered together, and upon such an occasion. But my sister and I durst not give way to it; for our father had often charged us in his lifetime, and upon his blessing, that no service should be at his burial. 'For,' said he, 'it will give occasion to speak some good things of me that I deserve not, and so false things will be uttered in this pulpit.' Mr. Ward rested satisfied, and did forbear. But the next Friday, at Ipswich, he turned his whole lecture into a funeral sermon for my father, in which he did lament and honour him, to the great satisfaction of the whole auditory.

I have now brought together all that I can discover about Samuel Ward's history. I heartily regret that the whole amount is so small, and that the facts recorded about him are so few. But we must not forget that the best part of Ward's life was spent in Suffolk, and that he seldom left his own beloved pulpit in St. Mary-le-Tower, Ipswich.[38] That he was well known by reputation beyond the borders of his own county, there can be no doubt. His selection to be a preacher at St. Paul's Cross in 1616, is a proof of this. But it is vain to suppose that the reputation of a preacher, however eminent, who lives and dies in a provincial town, will long survive him. In order to become the subject of biographies, and have the facts of his life continually noted down, a man must live in a metropolis. This was not Ward's lot; and, consequently, at the end of two hundred years, we seem to know little about him.

Ward's Sermons and Treatises

It only remains to say something about Ward's sermons and treatises, which have been lately, for the first time, reprinted, and made accessible to the modern reader of theology.[39] It must be distinctly understood that these reprints do not comprise the whole of Ward's writings. Beside these sermons and treatises, he wrote, in conjunction with Yates, a reply to Montague's famous book, *Appello Cæsarem*. There is also reason to think that he published one or two other detached sermons beside those which are now reprinted. I think, however, there can be little doubt that the nine sermons and treatises which have been lately republished by Mr. Nichol, are the only works of Samuel Ward which it would have been worthwhile to reprint, and in all probability the only works which he would have wished himself to be reproduced.

Of the merits of these sermons, the reading public will now be able to form an opinion. They were thought highly of in time past, and have received the commendation of very competent judges. Fuller testifies that

---

38 It seems that he expounded half the Bible during his ministry in Ipswich. See his preface to *The Happiness of Practice*.

39 Ward's sermons are to be found in Nichol's valuable series of reprints of Puritan divines, at the end of the third volume of Adams' works.

Ward "had a sanctified fancy, dexterous in designing expressive pictures, representing much matter in a little model." Doddridge says that Ward's "writings are worthy to be read through. His language is generally proper, elegant, and nervous. His thoughts are well digested, and happily illustrated. He has many remarkable veins of wit. Many of the boldest figures of speech are to be found in him, beyond any English writer, especially apostrophes, prosopopœias, dialogisms, and allegories."[40] This praise may at first sight seem extravagant. I shall, however, be disappointed if those who take the trouble to read Ward's writings do not think it well deserved.

It is only fair to Samuel Ward to remind the readers of his works, that at least three of the nine sermons and treatises now reprinted were not originally composed with a view to publication. The sermons entitled "A Coal from the Altar", "Balm from Gilead to Recover Conscience", and "Jethro's Justice of the Peace," would appear to have been carried through the press by friends and relatives. They have all the characteristics of compositions intended for ears rather than for eyes, for hearers rather than for readers. Yet I venture to say that they are three of the most striking examples of Ward's gifts and powers, out of the whole nine. The peroration of the sermon on conscience, in particular, appears to me one of the most powerful and effective conclusions to a sermon which I have ever read in the English language.[41]

The *doctrine* of Ward's sermons is always thoroughly Evangelical. He never falls into the extravagant language about repentance, which disfigures the writings of some of the Puritans. He never wearies us with the long supra-scriptural, systematic statements of theology, which darken the pages of others. He is always to the point, always about the main things in Divinity, and generally sticks to his text. To exalt the Lord Jesus Christ as high as possible, to cast down man's pride, to expose the sin-

---

40 How Doddridge could possibly have made the mistake of supposing that Ward died at the age of 28 is perfectly inexplicable!

41 The engraved title pages of two of the nine sermons, in the edition of 1636, are great curiosities in their way. The one which is prefixed to the *Woe to Drunkards* is intended to be a hit at the degeneracy of the times in which Ward lived. If it was really designed by Ward himself, it supplies some foundation for the rumour that he had a genius for caricaturing.

fulness of sin, to spread out broadly and fully the remedy of the gospel, to awaken the unconverted sinner and alarm him, to build up the true Christian and comfort him— these seem to have been objects which Ward proposed to himself in every sermon. And was he not right? Well would it be for the churches if we had more preachers like him!

The *style* of Ward's sermons is always eminently simple. Singularly rich in illustration, bringing everyday life to bear continually on his subject, pressing into his Master's service the whole circle of human learning, borrowing figures and similes from everything in creation, not afraid to use familiar language such as all could understand, framing his sentences in such a way that an ignorant man could easily follow him. Bold, direct, fiery, dramatic, and speaking as if he feared none but God— he was just the man to arrest attention, and to keep it when arrested, to set men thinking, and to make them anxious to hear him again. Quaint he is, undoubtedly, in many of his sayings. But he preached in an age when all were quaint, and his quaintness probably struck no one as remarkable. Faulty in taste he is, no doubt. But there never was the popular preacher against whom the same charge was not laid. His faults, however, were as nothing compared to his excellencies. Once more I say, well would it be for the churches if we had more preachers like him!

The *language* of Ward's sermons ought not to be passed over without remark. I venture to say, that in few writings of the seventeenth century will there be found so many curious, old-fashioned, and forcible words as in Ward's sermons. Some of these words are unhappily obsolete, and unintelligible to the multitude, to the grievous loss of English literature.

Extracts from Ward's Sermons

It only remains to give a few extracts from Ward's sermons which may give some idea of what this famous divine was as a preacher.

The first extract is from a sermon entitled "Christ is all in all."

> *All let Him be in all our thoughts and speeches. How happy were it if He were never out of our sight and minds, but that our souls were*

directed towards Him, and fixed on Him, as the sunflower towards the sun, the iron to the loadstone, the loadstone to the polestar. Hath He not for that purpose resembled Himself to all familiar and obvious objects:[42] to the light, that so often as we open our eyes we might behold Him; to bread, water, and wine, that in all our repasts we might feed on Him;[43] to the door, that in all our out and ingoing we might have Him in remembrance?

How happy if our tongues would ever run upon that name, which is honey in the mouth, melody in the ear, jubilee in the heart. Let the mariner prate of the winds, the merchant of his gain, the husbandman of his oxen.[44] Be thou a Pythagorean to all the world, and a Peripatetian to Christ; mute to all vanities, and eloquent only to Christ, that gave man his tongue and his speech. How doth Paul delight to record it, and harp upon it eleven times in ten verses, which Chrysostom first took notice of (1 Corinthians 1: 10).[45]

And how doth worthy Fox grieve to foresee and foretell that which we hear and see come to pass, that men's discourses would be taken up about trifles and nifles, as if all religion lay in the flight and pursuit of one circumstance or opinion; how heartily doth he pray, and vehemently wish that men would leave jangling about ceremonies, and spend their talk upon Him that is the substance; that learned men would write of Christ, unlearned men study of Him, preachers make Him the scope and subject of all their preaching.[46]

And what else, indeed, is our office but to elevate, not a piece of bread, as the Romish priests, but Christ in our doctrine; to travail in birth till He be formed in a people, to crucify Him in their eyes by lively preaching His death and passion. The old emblem of St. Christopher

---

42 Musculus et Brentius in Johannem. [The following footnotes seem to indicate the places where Ward claims to have found the ideas he uses in the sermon—*Editor*.]

43 Bernard.

44 Nolanus.

45 *In Præfat. ad Concionem de Christo crucifixo.*

46 Philip Melancthon in *Rhetor.*

is good, representing a preacher as one wading through the sea of this world, staying on the staff of faith, and lifting up Christ aloft to be seen of men. What else gained John the name of the Divine, and Paul of a wise master builder, but that he regarded not, as the fashion is nowadays, to have his reading, memory, and elocution, but Christ known, and Him crucified, and to build the Church skilfully, laying the foundation upon this Rock,[47] of which, if we hold our peace, the rocks themselves will cry. This being the sum of our art and task, by the help of Christ, to preach the gospel of Christ, to the praise of Christ, without whom a sermon is no sermon, preaching no preaching.[48]

The sum of the sum of all is, that the whole duty of all men is to give themselves wholly to Christ, to sacrifice not a leg, or an arm, or any other piece, but soul, spirit, and body, and all that is within us;[49] the fat, the inwards, the head and hoof, and all as a holocaust to Him, dedicating, devoting ourselves to His service all the days and hours of our lives, that all our days may be Lord's days. To whom, when we have so done, yet must we know we have given Him so much less than His due, as we worms and wretched sinners are less than the Son of God, who knew no sin.

To Him therefore let us live, to Him therefore let us die. So let us live to Him that we may die in Him, and breathe out our souls most willingly into His hands, with the like affection that John of Alexandria, surnamed the Almoner, for his bounty, is reported to have done, who, when he had distributed all he had to the poor, and made even with his revenues, as his fashion was yearly to do in his best health, thanked God he had now nothing left but his Lord and Master Christ, whom he longed to be with, and would now with unlimed and unentangled wings fly unto; or as, in fewer words, Peter of old and Lambert of later times, 'Nothing but Christ, nothing but Christ.' (Ward's **Sermons***, page 10 of the Nichol edition.)*

---

47 Lutherus.

48 Perkins in *Prophetica*.

49 Nazianzenus de Spiritu.

The second extract is from a sermon on Conscience, entitled "Balm from Gilead."

Hearken, O consciences! hear the word of the Lord. I call you to record this day, that it is your office to preach over our sermons again, or else all our sermons and labours are lost. You are the cuds of the soul, to chew over again. Against your reproofs, and against your secret and faithful admonitions, what exception can any take? Your balm is precious; your smitings break not the head, nor bring any disgrace. God hath given you a faculty to work wonders in private and solitude. Follow them home, therefore, cry aloud in their ears and bosoms, and apply what hath now and at other times been delivered.

Conscience, if the house and owner where thou dwellest be a son of peace, let thy peace and thy Master's peace abide and rest on him; that peace which the world never knows, nor can give, nor take away. Be thou propitious and benign, speak good things, cherish the least sparks and smoke of grace; if thou findest desire in truth, and in all things, bid them not fear and doubt of their election and calling. With those that desire to walk honestly, walk thou comfortably. Handle the tender and fearful gently and sweetly; be not rough and rigorous to them. Bind up the broken-hearted. Say unto them, 'Why art thou so disquieted and sad?' When thou seest them melancholy for losses and crosses, say unto them in cheer, as Elkanah to Hannah, 'What dost thou want? Am not I a thousand friends, wives, and children unto thee?'

Clap them on the back, hearten them in well-doing, spur them on to walk forward; yea, wind them up to the highest pitch of excellency, and then applaud them. Delight in the excellent of the earth.

Be a light to the blind and scrupulous.

Be a goad in the sides of the dull ones.

Be an alarm and trumpet of judgment to the sleepers and dreamers.

But as for the hypocrite, gall him and prick him at the heart. Let him well know that thou art God's spy in his bosom, a secret intelligencer, and wilt be faithful to God.

Bid the hypocrite walk 'in all things.'

Bid the civil add piety to charity.

Bid the wavering, inconstant, and licentious 'walk constantly.'

Bid the lukewarm and common Protestant for shame amend, be zealous, and 'walk honestly.'

But with the sons of Belial, the profane scorners, walk frowardly with them, haunt and molest them, give them no rest till they repent, be the gall of bitterness unto them. When they are swilling and drinking, serve them as Absalom's servants did Amnon, stab him at the heart. Yet remember, so long as there is any hope, that thine office is to be a pedagogue to Christ, to wound and kill, only to the end they may live in Christ, not so much to gaster and affright as to lead to Him; and, to that purpose, to be instant in season and out of season, that they may believe and repent.

But if they refuse to hear, and sin against thee, and the Holy Ghost also, then shake off the dust of thy feet, and either fall to torment them before their time, and drive them to despair; or if thou give them ease here, tell them thou wilt fly in their throat at the day of hearing when thou shalt and must speak, and they shall and must hear.

Conscience, thou hast commission to go into princes' chambers and council tables; be a faithful man of their counsel. Oh, that they would in all courts of Christendom set policy beneath thee, and make thee president of their councils, and hear thy voice, and not croaking Jesuits, sycophants, and liars. Thou mayest speak to them, subjects must pray for them, and be subject, for thy sake, to honour and obey them in the Lord.

Charge the courtiers not to trust in uncertain favours of princes, but to be trusty and faithful, as Nehemiah, Daniel, Joseph; whose histories pray them to read, imitate, and believe above Machiavelli's oracles.

Tell the foxes and politicians, that make the **main** the **by**, and the **by** the **main**, that an ill conscience hanged Ahithophel, overthrew Haman, Shebna, etc. Tell them it is the best policy, and Solomon's, who knew the best, to get and keep thy favour; to exalt thee, and thou shalt exalt them, be a shield to them, and make them as bold as the lion in the day of trouble, not fearing the envy of all the beasts of the forest, no, nor the roaring of the lion, in righteous causes.

Conscience, thou art the judge of judges, and shalt one day judge them; in the meanwhile, if they fear neither God nor man, be as the importunate widow, and urge them to do justice. Oh, that thou sattest highest in all courts, especially in such courts as are of thy jurisdiction, and receive their denomination from thee. Suffer not thyself to be exiled, make Felix tremble, discourse of judgment to them.

To the just judges, bid them please God and thee, and fear no other fear; assure them, for whatever they do of partiality or popularity, thou wilt leave them in the lurch; but what upon thy suit and command, thou will bear them out in it, and be their exceeding great reward.

If thou meetest in those courts and findest any such pleaders as are of thine acquaintance and followers, be their fee and their promoter. Tell them, if they durst trust thee, and leave Sunday works, bribing on both sides, selling of silence, pleading in ill causes, and making the law a nose of wax, if they durst plead all and only rightful causes, thou hast riches in one hand, and honour in the other, to bestow on them.

As for the tribe of Levi, there mayest thou be a little bolder, as being men of God, and men of conscience by profession. Be earnest with them to add **con** to their **science**, as a number to cyphers, that will make it something worth. Desire them to preach, not for filthy lucre or vain glory, but for thy sake: wish them to keep thee pure, and in thee to keep the mystery of faith; assure them thou art the only ship and cabinet of orthodoxal faith, of which, if they make shipwreck by laziness and covetousness, they shall be given over to Popery and Armin-

ianism, and lose the faith, and then write books of the apostasy, and intercession of faith, and a good conscience, which they never were acquainted withal, nor some drunkards of them ever so much as seemed to have." (Ward's **Sermons**, page 109 of the Nichol edition.)

I make no comment on the extracts I have given. I think they speak for themselves. No doubt tastes and opinions about sermons differ widely. But it is my own deliberate judgment, that a man who preaches in the style of Ward will never lack hearers.

4. William Gurnall

William Gurnall, Rector of Lavenham, in Suffolk, and author of *The Christian in Complete Armour*, is a man about whom the world possesses singularly little information. Perhaps there is no writer who has left a name so familiar to all readers of Puritan theology, but of whose personal history so little is known. Except the three facts—that he was a Puritan divine of the seventeenth century, that he was Minister of Lavenham, and that he wrote a well-known book of practical divinity—most persons know nothing of William Gurnall.

This dearth of information about so good a man appears at first sight extraordinary and unaccountable. Born, as he was, in a seaport town of no mean importance, the son of parents who held a prominent position in the town, educated at Cambridge, at one of the best known colleges of the day, the contemporary of leading divines of the Commonwealth times, minister of the largest church in West Suffolk for the uninterrupted period of thirty-five years, author of a work which, from its first appearance, was eminently popular, Gurnall is a man, we naturally feel, of whom more ought to be known. How is it then that more is not known? How shall we account for the absence of any notice of him in the biographical writings of his day?

I believe that these questions admit of a very simple answer. That answer is to be found in the line of conduct which Gurnall followed in the year 1662, on the passing of the unhappy Act of Uniformity. He did not secede from the Church of England! He was not one of the famous two thousand ministers who gave up their preferment on St. Bartholomew's Day, and became Nonconformists. He retained his position, and continued Rector of Lavenham. Puritan as he undoubtedly was, both in doctrine and practice, he did not do what many of his brethren did. When Baxter, Manton, Owen, Goodwin, and a host of other giants in theology, seceded from the Church of England, Gurnall stood fast, and refused to move. He did not act with the party with which he had generally acted, and was left behind.

The result of this line of conduct can easily be imagined. Whatever opinions we may hold about Gurnall's conformity, we must all allow that the course he took was not likely to make him a favourite with either of the two great religious parties into which England at that time was divided. A neutral is never popular in a season of strife and controversy. Both sides suspect him. Each party is offended at him for not casting his weight into their scale. This, I suspect, was precisely Gurnall's position. He was a Puritan in doctrine, and yet he steadfastly adhered to the Church of England. He was a minister of the Church of England, and yet a thorough Puritan both in preaching and practice. In fact, he was just the man to be disliked and slighted by both sides.

I throw out the conjecture I have made with considerable diffidence. It is undoubtedly nothing but a conjecture. But I look at the broad fact that the biographical writers who have handled Gurnall's age, have chronicled scores of names of far less weight than his, and have refused to say a word about the author of *The Christian in Complete Armour*. Calamy, Clarke, Neal, and Brooke have written hundreds of pages about men for whom the world cares nothing now, but not a page about Gurnall! I leave it to others to offer a better explanation of this fact, if they can. I must be allowed to retain my own settled conviction, that we should know far more about Gurnall if he had not submitted to the Act of Uniformity in 1662 and retained the pulpit of Lavenham parish church.

To supply a correct history of this good man and his times is the object of the biography I am now writing. Ever since I read *The Christian in Complete Armour* I have felt that the author of such a book was a man whose life ought to be known. From the day that I was transplanted into the Eastern Counties, and became a Suffolk incumbent, I have made it my business to study the lives of eminent Suffolk divines. None of them all appears to deserve excavation from undeserved oblivion so much as Gurnall.

The life of Gurnall

Almost the only source of information about Gurnall which we now possess is a small volume, published in 1830, by a writer named M'Keon, entitled, *An Inquiry into the Birthplace, Parentage, Life, and Writings of the Rev. William Gurnall, formerly Rector of Lavenham, in Suffolk, and author of 'The Christian in Complete Armour.'* This book was printed and published for the author at Woodbridge in Suffolk, and not in London. It is owing to this circumstance, perhaps, that it seems to have attracted little notice, and to have become comparatively unknown.

Mr. M'Keon was an inhabitant of Lavenham, and likely to procure information about Gurnall, if any one could. He was undoubtedly a painstaking man, and an antiquarian of considerable research. His accuracy and correctness are worthy of all commendation. There is hardly a single date or fact in his book which I have not taken the trouble to verify by inquiry and investigation; and there is hardly one, I feel bound to say, in which I have found him wrong. But it cannot be said that his *Inquiry* is written in a popular and attractive style. In accumulating facts he was most successful; in arranging and exhibiting them to the reading public I certainly think he failed.

However, whatever may be the faults of Mr. M'Keon's book, it is certainly the only attempt at any account of Gurnall which has hitherto existed. A funeral sermon, to be sure, was preached by Gurnall's friend and neighbour, the well-known commentator Burkitt; but the information it contains is comparatively very small. I must therefore frankly avow that I am indebted to Mr. M'Keon's work for the greater part of the facts about Gurnall which I have brought together in the following pages. I have tried to re-arrange these facts. I have endeavoured to present them to the reader in an attractive form, by illustrating them with some cross lights from the history of Gurnall's times. I have added a few facts which Mr. M'Keon was probably unable to obtain. But I think it only fair to state that Mr. M'Keon's book is the principal mine from which the biographical account of Gurnall now presented to the reader has been drawn. If I have added anything of interest to his work, it is almost always by following up clues which his volume indicated or put into my hand.

Early Days

William Gurnall was born at Lynn, in the county of Norfolk, in the year 1616, and was baptized at St. Margaret's church in that town, on the 17th November 1616. His father and mother were married at St. Margaret's church on the 31st December 1615, and the subject of this memoir was therefore their eldest child.[50]

It has often been observed that the mothers of great men, and especially of great divines, have been remarkable for strong mind and force of intellect. Mothers have been found, as a general rule, to influence children's character far more than fathers. How far this was true in the case of Gurnall we have, unfortunately, no means of judging. We only know that his mother's maiden name was Catherine Dressit, and that in all probability she was a native of Lynn.

Gregory, the father of William Gurnall, appears to have been one of the principal inhabitants of Lynn. At any rate he was an Alderman of his native town in the year when his son was born, and was Mayor of

---

50 Mr. Hankinson, once Rector of St. Margaret's, Lynn, informed me that the name "Gurnall," to the best of his knowledge, is no longer known in Lynn. But he says that the name "Curling" is not uncommon, and that he has little doubt it was originally "Gurnal." He adds, "I find an entry of baptism in 1799, where the name is 'Gurnell or Gurling.'" In Suffolk, the names of "Girling" and "Grinling," as I happen to know from the parish register of Stradbroke, are very common.

the borough eight years afterwards, in 1624. Nothing is known of his calling or occupation. The fact that his son died possessed of certain landed property at Walpole, a country parish not far from Lynn, makes it highly probable that Gregory Gurnall was a landed proprietor. But on this point again nothing certain is known.

Gurnall had the misfortune to lose his father when he was only fifteen years old. His death is recorded in the register of St. Margaret's, Lynn, as having taken place on the 14th October 1631. He was buried in St. Margaret's church, and a tomb was erected to his memory, with a curious inscription. This tomb is no longer extant, as the spire of St. Margaret's church was blown down in a violent hurricane in the year 1741 and, falling on the body of the church, destroyed a large portion of the building. Mackerell's *History of Lynn*, published about four years before the hurricane, records the inscription. If epitaphs were worth anything, the language of Gregory Gurnall's epitaph might lead us to the conclusion that he was a godly man. But unhappily it is too well known that tombstones are not always to be trusted.

How long Gurnall's mother survived his father there is no evidence to show. M'Keon conjectures that she married again. It is certainly a curious fact that Burkitt, the commentator, in his funeral sermon on William Gurnall, uses the following language: "How great was that tribute of veneration and respect which he constantly paid to the hoary hairs of his aged parents!" Considering that his father died when he was only fifteen years old, these words can hardly be supposed to apply to Gregory Gurnall. Unless therefore the word "parents" in Burkitt's sermon is a printer's mistake for "parent", it seems a very probable idea that Gurnall's mother married again, and that he had a kind and loving step-father. But who he was, and how long his mother lived, we do not know.

Adolescence and Education

The first fifteen years of Gurnall's life appear to have been spent in his native town of Lynn. There is, at any rate, no doubt that he was educated at the Free Grammar School of that town up to the time when he went to Cambridge. The fact is recorded in the books of the school.

The first fifteen years of life have often so much weight in the formation of a man's character, that it would be very interesting to find out the influences under which William Gurnall spent his early years. Unhappily we possess no materials for doing this. Ambrose Fish was appointed Master of Lynn Grammar School in 1626, in the place of Mr. Robinson, deceased, and Robert Woodmansea was appointed Master in 1627. But we know nothing of these men. I can only point out two things which appear to me deserving of attention.

For one thing, we may probably trace up to Lynn Gurnall's Puritan predilections and opinions. Lynn was one of the chief towns of the most thoroughly Protestant district in England in the seventeenth century. In the days of Queen Mary and Elizabeth the inhabitants of Norfolk and Suffolk were famous for their deep attachment to the doctrines of the Reformation. In the days of the Stuarts and the Commonwealth they were no less famous for their steadfast adherence to Puritan principles. In no part of England were High Church opinions so thoroughly disliked as in the diocese of Norwich, and in no diocese were the minds of people so continually exasperated by vexatious persecutions of Nonconformists.[51]

Brought up in a large market town like Lynn, we cannot doubt that the religious atmosphere m which young Gurnall moved was essentially Puritan. If, as it seems not unlikely from a comparison of dates, the famous John Arrowsmith and Samuel Fairclough were Ministers at Lynn during Gurnall's school days, we get an additional ray of light thrown on the source of his doctrinal opinions. To hear men like Arrowsmith and Fairclough preach every Sunday, and perhaps to be solemnly catechised or examined by Arrowsmith on stated public occasions, were just the things likely to produce an indelible impression on a mind like Gurnall's.[52]

---

51 Harsnet, White, Corbet, Wren, and Montague were Bishops of Norwich between 1619 and 1641. Three of them, at least, viz., Harsnet, Wren, and Montague, were notoriously very High Churchmen, and strongly opposed to the Puritans.

52 John Arrowsmith was born at Gateshead, in 1602. He was educated at St. John's College,

For another thing, we probably owe to Gurnall's early residence at Lynn his remarkable familiarity with the sea, sailors, and shipping. I was once puzzled to make out the reason why nautical illustrations so frequently occur in his writings. It did not surprise me to find an author like Gurnall, who delighted in illustrations, pressing everything in town and country into his service. I could understand the man who was Rector of a Suffolk town for thirty-five years drawing comparisons from shops, and farms, and streets, and fields, and horses, and cattle, and corn, and grass, and flowers. I could understand the minister who lived through the bloody wars of the Commonwealth times using abundant imagery from the habits of soldiers, and from the battle-field. But I never could understand Gurnall's familiarity with the sea and shipping, until I found out that he was born and bred in Lynn.

He knew well what a sailor's life was. He had seen the quaint-looking craft which carried on the coasting trade of Lynn. He had doubtless talked with sailors who could tell the perils of "the Wash," the Lincolnshire coast, the Norfolk Sands, and the Voyage to the Humber. Hence came his nautical illustrations in Lavenham pulpit. How true it is that

---

Cambridge, and was chosen Fellow of Katherine Hall. He was elected one of the University Preachers, was beneficed at Lynn, and was afterwards Preacher at St. Margaret's, Ironmonger's Lane, London. He was a leading member of the Westminster Assembly, and had a principal share in drawing up the Assembly's Catechism. He was elected Master of St. John's College in 1644, and was chosen Vice-Chancellor of Cambridge in 1647. In 1651 he was appointed Regius Professor of Divinity, and Rector of Somersham. He was chosen Master of Trinity College in 1653, died in 1659, and was buried in Trinity College Chapel. His commentary on the first seventeen verses of the first chapter of St. John's Gospel, entitled, *God-Man*, gives a very favourable impression of his ability.

Samuel Fairclough was born at Haverhill in 1594, and was educated at Queen's College, Cambridge. He was appointed Lecturer at Lynn by the Mayor and Aldermen in 1619, and continued there, according to Samuel Clarke who gives a long and most interesting account of him, "for some time." The opposition and persecution of Harsnet, Bishop of Norwich, obliged him to resign this lecture. He was afterwards Lecturer at Clare, in Suffolk, and was then appointed Rector of Keddington by Sir N. Barnardiston. He resigned this living in 1662, on account of the Act of Uniformity. He died in retirement in 1677, aged 84. Though a retiring man, and not known by any writings, he seems to have been a man of singular gifts and graces. There is an interesting tablet in Heveningham Church, erected by his daughter, wife of Mr. Jones, Rector of Heveningham. He lived at Heveningham for two years, but died at Stowmarket.

all knowledge is useful to a minister of Christ! The man of God makes everything he has seen become serviceable to his Master's cause.

Emmanuel College, Cambridge

The next thing that we know about Gurnall is his connection with Cambridge as a pensioner of Emmanuel College. It appears that Lynn Corporation had two Scholarships at Emmanuel in its gift, connected with the Grammar School of the town. To one of these Gurnall was presented by the Corporation, in December, 1631, not long after his father's death. A correspondent of M'Keon, at Lynn, says, "I find, on reference to the Corporation books, that on the 2nd December 1631, William Gurnall, son of Gregory Gurnall, Alderman there, lately deceased, and one of the scholars of Lynn School, was nominated to one of the Scholarships in Emmanuel College, Cambridge, called Lynn Scholarship, or Mr. Titley's Scholarship; and that on the 11th June 1632, the nomination, dated 29th March, then last, passed the Corporation seal."

Of Gurnall's history during his residence at Cambridge we know literally nothing, with the exception of the following bald facts. The College books record that William Gurnall, pensioner, of Norfolk, was admitted March 29th 1632, was B.A., 1635, and M.A., 1639. It is certain that he was never elected a Fellow of his College, and as the Lynn Scholarship was only tenable for seven years, it is highly probable that he ceased to reside at Cambridge in the year 1639, when he took his degree as M.A. and received no further assistance from his Scholarship.

It would, no doubt, be highly interesting if we knew something of Gurnall's history during the seven years of his University life. The character of a young man is generally moulded for life during the period between sixteen and twenty-three, and the author of *The Christian in Complete Armour* was probably no exception to this rule. Who were his friends and companions? Who were his tutors and lecturers? Was he a reading man? Whom did he walk with, and talk with? What great preachers did he hear in the University pulpit? What were his habits and ways of employing his time? What side did he espouse in the mighty controversies of the day? All these are questions which it would be very pleasant to have answered. The answers would throw great light on many a passage in his after-life and writings. But the answers, unhappily, are not forthcoming. The only light that we can throw on Gurnall's University life consists of a few facts about his College, and the general state of England between 1632 and 1639.

The College to which Gurnall belonged was always famous in the seventeenth century for its theological tendencies. It was eminently a Puritan College.

Sir Walter Mildmay, of Chelmsford in Essex, was the founder of Emmanuel College, and even from its very foundation in 1585, it seems to have been notorious for its attachment to Puritan principles. Fuller, in his *History of Cambridge*, relates that on "Sir Walter Mildmay coming to Court, soon after he had founded his College, Queen Elizabeth said to him, 'Sir Walter, I hear you have erected a Puritan foundation.' 'No, madam,' saith he, 'far be it from me to countenance anything contrary to your established laws; but I have set an acorn, which, when it becomes an oak, God alone knows what will be the fruit thereof.' Sure I am (adds Fuller, writing about 1650) at this day it hath overshadowed all the University, more than a moiety of the present Masters of Colleges being bred therein."

The number of leading divines of the seventeenth century who were educated at Emmanuel College, Cambridge, is certainly extraordinary. Beside Bishop Hall and Bishop Bedell, we find in the list of its members the names of Stephen Marshall, Jeremiah Burroughs, Thomas Sheppard, Thomas Hooker, Ezekiel Culverwell, Ralph Cudworth, Samuel Crooke, John Cotton, John Stoughton, Anthony Burgess, Laurence Chaderton, John Preston, Anthony Tuckney, Lazarus Seaman, Matthew Poole, Samuel Clarke, Ralph Venning, Thomas Watson, Stephen Charnock, William Bridge, Peter Sterry, Samuel Cradock. Any one familiar with Puritan divinity will see at a glance that this catalogue embraces the names of some of the most eminent Puritan writers. Some of them, no doubt, were contemporaries and fellow-students of Gurnall himself.

From inquiries which I have made, I have succeeded in obtaining some information about Emmanuel College between the years 1632 and 1639, which I think will not be devoid of interest to all admirers of Gurnall. At any rate it will show who were at Emmanuel when he was there, both as an undergraduate and a graduate, and with what kind of minds he was associated.

The Masters at Emmanuel in Gurnall's time were (1) William Sancroft, uncle of the Archbishop, who held the office from 1628 to 1637; and (2) Holdsworth, who held the office from 1637 to 1645, when he was ejected by the Earl of Manchester. He was a zealous advocate of the King, and attended him during his confinement in the Isle of Wight, and soon after, according to Neal, died of grief.

The reason why Gurnall was never elected Fellow of his College was probably, if I may venture a conjecture, the high character and attainments of his competitors. According to the books of Emmanuel, Ralph Cudworth was elected Fellow in 1639, Worthington (afterward Master of Jesus) in 1641, and Sancroft (afterward Archbishop of Canterbury) in 1642.

The Fellows of Emmanuel between 1632 and 1639 were the following: Walter Foster, Richard Clarke, John Ward, Thomas Ball, Ezekiel Wright, Thomas Hill, Nicholas Hall, William Bridge, Samuel Bowles, Henry Salmon, David Ensigne, Anthony Burgess, Thomas Holbeck, Thomas Horton, Malachi Harris, R. Sorsby, Benjamin Whichcot, John Henderson, John Almond, R. Weller, Peter Sterry, Laurence Sarson, John Saddler, Ralph Cudworth.

"All the Fellows," says a member of Emmanuel, "appear to have been tutors in their day, though some had more pupils than others. As far as our books lead us to infer, Hill, Hall, Burgess, Holbeck, Ensigne, Salmon, Whichcot, all seem to have been most popular tutors in their day. We have no tutors' books which tell us under whom Gurnall was admitted."

When I add to the above information the fact that Horrox, the astronomer, was admitted at Emmanuel in 1632, the same year as Gurnall, and that Archbishop Sancroft, the famous nonjuror, was admitted in 1633,

I shall have exhausted all the stock of information that I have been able to scrape together about Gurnall's College life and his contemporaries.

Seven years spent at a College like Emmanuel could not fail to have an effect on Gurnall's mind. Brought up from his boyhood to honour and reverence the Puritans as the excellent of the earth, at Lynn, trained afterwards at a College where the whole atmosphere was peculiarly Puritan, it would have been strange indeed if Gurnall had grown up without decided Puritan opinions.

The state of England during the seven years of Gurnall's University life was very peculiar. It was the crisis of the troubled period between the Reformation and the Commonwealth times. The suicidal and blind misgovernment of Charles I was rapidly paving the way for the destruction of the throne. The undisguised Romish tendencies and bitter persecutions of Archbishop Laud and his fellow-workers were doing the same for the Church of England. From one end of the country to the other there were discontent, murmuring, controversy, bitterness, and party spirit. On every side there were symptoms of a coming break-up, or a violent conflict both in Church and State.

Cambridge, we need not doubt, had its full share of all the troubles and discomfort of this stormy period. The following passage from Fuller's *History of Cambridge* records things which happened there in 1632, the very year that Gurnall entered Emmanuel, things which, no doubt, he saw with his own eyes and heard with his own ears:—

> *This year, a grave divine, preaching before the University at St. Mary's, had this passage in his sermon: 'That as at the Olympian games he was counted the conqueror who could drive his chariot wheels nearest to the mark, yet so as not to hinder his running, or stick thereon, so he, who in his sermons could preach near Popery, and yet no Popery, there was your man.' And, indeed, it now began to be the complaint of most moderate men, that many in the University, both in school and pulpit, approached the opinion of the Church of Rome more than ever before.*

> Mr. Bernard, Lecturer of St. Sepulchre's in London, preached at St. Mary's in the afternoon of May 6th, his text, 1 Sam. iv. 21: 'The glory is departed from Israel,' etc. In handling whereof he let fall some passages which gave distaste to a prevalent party in the University, as for saying: (1) That God's ordinances, when blended and adultered with innovations of men, cease to be God's ordinances, and He owneth them no longer. (2) That it is impossible any should be saved, living and dying without repentance, in the doctrine of Rome, as the Tridentine Council hath decreed it. (3) That treason is not limited to the blood royal; but that he is a traitor against a nation that depriveth it of God's ordinances. (4) That some shamefully symbolize in Pelagian error and superstitious ceremonies with the Church of Rome. Let us pray such to their conversion or to their destruction, etc.
>
> Dr. Cumber, Vice-Chancellor, gave speedy notice hereof to Dr. Laud, Bishop of London, though he (so quick his University intelligence) had information thereof before. Therefore he was brought into the High Commission, and a recantation tendered to him, which he refused to subscribe, though professing his sincere sorrow and penitency, in his petition and letter to the Bishop, for any oversight and unbecoming expression in his sermon. Hereupon he was sent back to the new prison, where he died. If he was miserably abused therein by his keepers, as some have reported, to the shortening of his life, He that maketh inquisition for blood, either hath, or will be, a revenger thereof.

This deplorable affair took place, let us remember, in the year 1632, the very year that Gurnall came up to reside at Emmanuel. How much stir it would excite among the undergraduates of a thoroughly Puritan College we can easily imagine. All who know anything of an English University, know how ready undergraduates are, as a body, to sympathize with the persecuted and oppressed, and to side with the minority.

It was during Gurnall's residence at Cambridge that Dr. Ward, one of the representatives of the Church of England at the Synod of Dort, gave the following unsatisfactory description of the state of the University, in a letter to Archbishop Usher, dated 1634. He says, "It may be you are willing to hear of our University affairs. I may truly say I never knew them in worse condition since I was a member thereof, which is almost forty-six years."[53]

It was during Gurnall's residence at Cambridge that the infamous sentence on Prynne, Bastwick, and Burton, was passed in the Court of Star Chamber. For publishing certain alleged libels on the Church of England these unfortunate men were condemned to stand in the pillory, and have their ears publicly cut off. The sentence was actually carried into effect, June 30th 1637, in Palace Yard. Bastwick was a physician, who had been educated at Emmanuel College. We can easily imagine the sensation which his punishment would create within the walls of his old College.

It was during Gurnall's residence at Cambridge that the famous disturbances in Scotland arose, out of Archbishop Laud's attempt to introduce the notorious Scotch Liturgy, with its Popish Communion Office, into the Churches of Edinburgh. The well-known riot in St. Giles' Church, when a stool is said to have been thrown at the Bishop of Edinburgh's head by a zealous woman called Jenny Geddes, took place on Sunday July 23rd 1637.

It was during Gurnall's residence at Cambridge that John Hampden began the unhappy struggle between the King and his subjects by refusing to pay ship-money. The decision of the Chief Justice was given against him on the 9th June 1637.

I mention these facts and dates in order to give the reader some idea of the times in which Gurnall passed through his University career. We cannot doubt that his character and opinions must have been strongly influenced by them. No one could be at Cambridge from 1632 to 1639 without seeing and hearing things which would leave a mark on his memory for life, and without coming across a stream of conflicting opinions which he would remember to his dying day. No doubt Gurnall became acquainted with some of the best specimens of the Puritan divines.

---

53 Usher's *Correspondence*, No. 179.

No doubt also he saw in the heart of a Puritan College enough to make him feel that all Puritans were not perfect men. I venture the conjecture that his after-life at every step was greatly influenced by the recollection of what he saw at Emmanuel, Cambridge.

Life after Cambridge

The five years of Gurnall's life immediately after he left Cambridge, in 1639, are a period in his history of which nothing whatever seems to be known. I must honestly confess that I can throw little light upon it, and can only offer surmises and conjectures. He disappears from our notice on leaving Emmanuel, in 1639. He does not appear again till he is made Rector of Lavenham, in 1644. But how, and where, and in what manner, and in what official capacity he spent the intervening interval of five years we have no certain record.

It would be difficult to name five years of English history in which so many important events occurred, as between 1639 and 1644. Within these five years the famous Long Parliament commenced its sittings, the no less famous Westminster Assembly of divines was convened, Lord Strafford was beheaded, Archbishop Laud committed to prison, and the Courts of High Commission and Star Chamber abolished. Within these five years the civil war between the King and the Parliament actually broke out, the standard was raised at Nottingham, the battles of Edgehill, Newbury, and Marston Moor were fought, and Hampden, Pym, and Lord Falkland were all laid in their graves. Last, but not least, the *Solemn League and Covenant* was subscribed by the adherents of the Parliament side, in which, among other things, they pledged themselves to "endeavour the extirpation of Popery and Prelacy: that is, Church government by archbishops, bishops, their chancellors and commissaries, deans and chapters, archdeacons, and all other ecclesiastical officers depending on that hierarchy."

And what was Gurnall doing all these five years? We cannot tell. Perhaps he was staying quietly with his friends at Lynn. Perhaps he was hearing and learning what he could in London. Perhaps he was turning to account his University education by acting as tutor to some noble or wealthy family, as many young divines did in that day. These are idle conjectures after all. There are only two facts that we know about him. One is that he must have been ordained some time between 1639 and 1644. The other is that he must have preached at Sudbury within this period. This last point is made clear by his own words, in a letter addressed to Sir Symond D'Ewes, in which he speaks of the Sudbury people making difficulties about his removal to Lavenham.

Gurnall's Ordination

The subject of Gurnall's entrance into the ministry is shrouded in complete obscurity. There is no one point in his personal history about which we know so little. When he was ordained, where he was ordained, to what cure of souls he was ordained, by whom he was ordained, whether he was first ordained by Episcopal or by Presbyterian ordination, are things about which we are entirely in the dark. After a good deal of troublesome research and investigation into the subject, I must honestly confess that I can find out nothing about it. I have only discovered, by the kindness of the present Bishop of Norwich and the late Bishop of Ely, that his name does not appear in the ordination registers of Norwich and Ely between 1639 and 1644.

It is, of course, possible that he was ordained by the bishop of some other diocese, though even then it is certain that he was only ordained deacon. But it is far more probable that he entered the ministry without receiving Episcopal orders at all. Most likely he was set apart for the work as a Presbyterian Minister, by "the laying on of the hands of the Presbytery."

I am not disposed to waste the reader's time by entering into any discussion of the comparative merits of Episcopal and Presbyterian orders, though, of course, I have my own opinions as a conscientious Episcopalian. I only venture the remark, that we have no right to infer anything as to Gurnall's opinions about Episcopacy, from his want of Episcopal orders. We must remember the peculiar times in which he entered the ministry. There was probably no alternative left to him. He must either have been ordained by Presbyterian ordination, or not have been ordained at all.

The plain truth is, that the times when Gurnall entered the ministry were times of disorder and confusion. It was a period of transition. Everything that had been settled and established in Church and State was being pulled to pieces. They were strange times, and strange things happened in them. We may well expect to find that there were all sorts of irregularities and diversities of practice about ordination.

Bishop Hall, in his famous account of himself, called *His Hard Measure*, makes the following statement, which deserves the more notice because he was Bishop of Norwich, and Lavenham was then in his diocese. He says, "After the Covenant was appointed to be taken (September 26th 1643), and was generally swallowed of both clergy and laity, my power of *ordination* was with some violence restrained. For when I was going on in my wonted course, which no law or ordinance had inhibited, certain forward volunteers in the city, banding together, stirred up the mayor, and aldermen, and sheriffs (of Norwich), to call me to an account for an open violation of their Covenant."

> To this purpose, divers of them came to my gate at a very unseasonable time, and knocking very vehemently, required to speak with the Bishop. Messages were sent to them to know their business; nothing would satisfy them but the Bishop's presence. At last I came down to them, and demanded what the matter was; they would have the gate opened, and then they would tell me. I answered that I would know them better first; if they had anything to say to me I was ready to hear them. They told me they had a writing for me from the Mayor and some other of their magistrates. The paper contained both a challenge of me for breaking the Covenant, in ordaining ministers, and withal required me to give in the names of those which were ordained by me both then and formerly since the Covenant. My answer was that the

> Mayor was much abused by those who had misinformed him and drawn that paper from him; that I would the next day give a full answer to the writing. They moved that my answer might be my personal appearance at the guildhall. I asked them when they ever heard of a Bishop of Norwich appearing before a Mayor. I knew mine own place, and would take that way of answer which I thought fit, and so dismissed them, who had given out that day, that had they known before of mine ordaining, they would have pulled me and those whom I ordained out of the chapel by the ears."[54]

Let us add to this curious testimony the following passage from Neal, the well-known historian of the Puritans. He says, "From the time of taking the Covenant (September 28th 1643), we may date the entire dissolution of the hierarchy, though it was not as yet abolished by an ordinance of Parliament. There were no ecclesiastical courts, no visitations, no wearing the habits, no regard paid to the canons or ceremonies, or even to the Common Prayer." He says immediately afterwards: "Upon the sitting of the Assembly of Divines all church worship went through their hands. The parishes elected their ministers. The Assembly examined and approved of them, and the Parliament confirmed them in their benefices without any regard to the Archbishop or his vicar. Thus the Earl of Manchester filled the vacant pulpits in the associated counties."[55]

After reading these passages we may well understand why there is no record of Gurnall's ordination as Deacon in the Registers of Norwich or Ely. He began his ministry in the diocese of Norwich, and was an inhabitant of one of the most thoroughly Puritan districts of the seven "associated counties." Whether be desired Episcopal Ordination or not we do not know, though his subsequent ordination by Bishop Reynolds, at a later period of his ministry, ought not to be forgotten. But it is highly probable that at the time when be entered the ministry he could not have received Episcopal Ordination even if he had wished it.

---

54 Hall's *Works*, Volume 1, page 54 (P. Hall's Edition).

55 Neal's *History*, Volume 3, pages 79-80 (Toulmin's Edition).

The matter, after all, is not one of primary importance. The Divine right of Episcopacy, to the exclusion of all other forms of Church government, and the absolute necessity of Episcopal Ordination to make a right minister of Christ, are positions that cannot be established from Scripture. The 23rd Article of the Church of England has exhibited a wise moderation in handling the whole question. It says: "It is not lawful for any man to take upon him the office of public preaching, or ministering the Sacrament in the congregation, before he be lawfully called and sent to execute the same." But the Article cautiously avoids defining too closely what are valid orders. It goes on: "Those we ought to judge lawfully called and sent, which be chosen and called to the work by men who have public authority given unto them in the congregation to call and send ministers into the Lord's vineyard." This, we need not doubt, was Gurnall's position. Episcopal Ordination he probably did not receive on entering the ministry, and most likely could not have obtained it. But that he was "lawfully called and sent into the Lord's vineyard" we need not doubt, though in all probability it was only "by laying on of the hands of the Presbytery."

Minister of Lavenham

We now come to the most important event in Gurnall's life, and the one which fixed him down in one spot for the remaining thirty-five years of his life. That event was his appointment to be Minister of the parish of Lavenham in Suffolk. This, it appears, happened about the month of December 1644, when he was twenty-eight years old.

The manner of Gurnall's appointment was somewhat singular, and curiously illustrative of the strange and troublesome times in which it took place. Sir Symond D'Ewes, the famous antiquary, was patron of the living of Lavenham, and chief proprietor in the parish. It appears that he gave the living to Gurnall at the request of the parishioners, and the appointment was ratified by order of the House of Commons.

The order of the House of Commons is so peculiar a document, that

I venture to transcribe it whole and entire, as M'Keon gives it, from an extract from the Journals of the House, furnished to him by the Clerk of the Journals.

16°- Decembris, 1644, 20 Car. 1.

Lavenham Rectory

WHEREAS *the Church of Lavenham, in the county of Suffolk, lately became void by the decease of Ambrose Coppinger, Doctor of Divinity, and that Sir Symond D'Ewes, patron of the said Church, hath conferred the advowson of the same upon William Gurnall, Master of Arts, a learned, godly, and orthodox divine:*

It is ordered by the House of Commons that the said William Gurnall shall be, and continue, Rector and Incumbent of the same Church during the term of his natural life, and shall have, receive, and enjoy all such tithes, as other Rectors and Incumbents of same Church before him have had, received, and enjoyed. Provided always that the same William Gurnall do pay upon his avoidance all such first fruits and tithes unto his Majesty, as by the laws of this realm are, and shall be due from time to time."[56]

A careful reader can hardly fail to notice some amusing points in this document. The right of Sir Symond D'Ewes to present is stated and allowed, and yet the presentation must be ratified by the order of the House of Commons! Gurnall's qualifications are broadly stated. The House declares him to be "learned, godly, and orthodox!" The King's name is carefully brought in (though the Parliament was at open war with him), and provision is inserted for the payment of first fruits to his Majesty! The name, office, and authority of the Bishop of Norwich, in whose diocese Lavenham was, are as utterly ignored as if they had never existed! Truly we may say that Gurnall lived in strange times!

What chain of providential circumstances led Gurnall to a town in the

---

56 Volume 3, page 725. The same record of Gurnall's presentation, word for word, is to be found in the Norwich Register of Institutions, No. 24, 1638—1648.

south-west corner of Suffolk, after leaving Cambridge, we do not know. Why the good man should turn up at Sudbury and Lavenham, five years after leaving Emmanuel, is a point which must be left to conjecture. We know nothing certain about it. It is, however, not unworthy of notice, that there was a certain James Gurnall living at Lavenham in 1644, who had a daughter baptized there on the 4th September in that year. It is by no means improbable, as M'Keon suggests, that this James Gurnall was a relative of the Gurnalls of Lynn, and that the relationship was the cause of William Gurnall visiting Lavenham, and becoming known in the neighbourhood.

It is also worthy of notice that Henry Coppinger, who died Rector of Lavenham in 1622, and was father of Gurnall's predecessor, Ambrose Coppinger, was connected by marriage with Gurnall's native place, Lynn. It is stated on a monument erected to his memory in Lavenham Church, that he married Ann, daughter of Henry Fisher, of Lynn, in Norfolk. Lynn was not so large a place that the families of Gurnall and Mr. Coppinger would not be acquainted with one another, and this may have been another cause of his settling in Lavenham. These are, of course, only conjectures, but I think them worth mentioning, and they must be taken for what they are worth.

How Gurnall became acquainted with Sir Symond D'Ewes, and whether he was appointed by him to the Rectory of Lavenham on public or private grounds, we have no means of ascertaining. A statement, quoted by M'Keon from a manuscript in Herald's College, by Mr. Appleton, about Suffolk, is manifestly a mistake. He says Sir Symond D'Ewes "freely and very willingly gave the Rectory of Lavenham unto Mr. William Gurnall, now Incumbent there, although to him then unknown, at the request of the parish, which hath been much for the benefit of the town in many ways." Appleton was clearly misinformed here. There is a correspondence extant in the Harleian MSS. between Gurnall and Sir Symond D'Ewes, of which the first letter is dated March 1644. Beside this, Sir Symond was elected M.P. for Sudbury in 1640, and resided in the parish of Lavenham, so that he could hardly fail to know something about Gurnall.

The correspondence between Gurnall and Sir Symond D'Ewes, to which reference has been made, is a curiosity in its way. It consists of eight Latin letters, composed in the most approved classical style, and affording evidence that Gurnall was a tolerably good Latin scholar. Judged by the standard of modern times the matter of these letters is not much to be admired. There is a tone of obsequiousness and flattery about them which to our eyes seems very unworthy of a Christian, and very unlike what we should have expected from a Puritan. But it is only fair to remember the fashion of Gurnall's age. Dedications and letters to public men in the seventeenth century are often stuffed with high-flown language and hyperbolic compliments. It was as common to write in such a strain as it is for us to sign ourselves "your obedient servant." The words meant nothing, and were only used because it was the custom to use them. If Gurnall had not written his Latin letters to Sir Symond D'Ewes in a very verbose, extravagant, and complimentary style, he would probably have been set down as an illiterate and unpolished man.

Some account of the contents of these eight letters will perhaps be found interesting. They throw a little light, at any rate, on Gurnall's presentation to Lavenham; and if we knew the meaning of the allusions which they contain, we should understand a good deal better than we do now the history of his settlement in the place with which his name is inseparably connected.[57]

The first letter is dated Lavenham, March 26th 1644. It is a petition on behalf of a man who had been wounded in the service of the State and appears to have been bearer of the letter. It contains some general remarks on the discredit thrown upon religion when wounded soldiers are neglected, and on the duty of providing them with comfortable maintenance. Beside this, there is nothing worth notice.

The second letter is dated July 24th 1644. It is endorsed "to the Right Worthy Sir Symond D'Ewes, at his lodgings in Margaret's, Westminster." The place from which it is written is not stated. In this letter for

---

57 As a general rule, I have given the letters as translated by M'Keon. In a few instances I have attempted to mend his translation.

the first time the subject of Gurnall's appointment to Lavenham is mentioned. There seems to have been some difficulty about the matter, which at this distance of time we cannot, of course, explain. The letter was evidently written while the difficulty was pending. It contains the following passage, which I give in M'Keon's translation in its entirety:—

> I have received your letter breathing nothing but love, and should immediately have answered it, had I not been called into Norfolk on public business. On my return I promised myself some certain grounds for a reply. But alas! the knot which I left to be untied I found still more perplexed and involved, so that I appeared, like the ship of St. Paul, to have 'fallen into a place where two seas met' [Acts 27:41]. While my mind is fixed on Lavenham, there threatens a storm at Sudbury, which accuses me of being lured by a golden bait. But were I to refuse this Providence held out to me by your hands, I might, not unjustly, appear disobedient to God, and ungrateful to you who offer it to me. In such a storm a skilful pilot (I mean Solomon) suggested to me, 'in the multitude of counsellors there is safety' [Proverbs 11:14]. Most willingly, therefore, did I submit the hearing and determining the whole cause to certain ministers in my neighbourhood. If I must die, I could wish it should be in the hands of the most skilful physicians; if I must err, I should wish it to be among men most famous for their learning and piety. In a short time I hope to finish this whole business, and then I will write again to your honour.

This is a curious letter. One would like to know what was the knotty point which Gurnall could not untie, and who were the "certain ministers" whom he consulted. One thing, at any rate, it helps to confirm. It seems to indicate that Gurnall was a minister at Sudbury before he was Rector of Lavenham. Yet it is a singular fact, that at the present time no inhabitant of Sudbury, to whom I have applied, seems to know anything about Gurnall's connection with the town.

The third letter is dated Sudbury, September 1st 1644. At the time when it was written it was evidently a settled thing, that Gurnall should have the living of Lavenham, though the appointment was not yet completed. Amidst a quantity of verbose and fulsome compliments, which can only be excused by the customs of Gurnall's day, the following paragraphs are worth quoting:

> I firmly believe, most worshipful, that the only happiness which you hope or wish for in this filthy world is that of doing good. In this humble and grateful disposition, therefore, you may triumph that the numerous population of Lavenham now enjoy under your shadow the gospel.
>
> If God should bless my slender labours, whatever they may be, as many as may be imbued with Divine light, or cherished with its dew, will be a solace, and even a crown to you, under whose shield I fight. Happy indeed, still more and more, might we have had the English nation, which we now see so universally torn by civil wars, if with the same care with which you have laboured, all our patrons had striven in the propagation of the gospel. But, alas, many make market of the souls of others while they peril their own! This will redound to your great honour. Not less do you strive to give than others to sell the priesthood.

The postscript to this letter is curious. Gurnall says, "One thing at the end of your letter I had almost forgot. You therein just mention the Bishop. My doubts increase as to the propriety of going to him, particularly since the opinions both of the clergy and of the people have become known to me."

The fourth letter is dated Lavenham, October 26th 1644. It is a complimentary letter written on the occasion of Sir Symond D'Ewes giving Gurnall a copy of some antiquarian work he had lately published. It contains no allusion to the subject of the living of Lavenham, and there is nothing in it worth quoting.

The fifth letter is dated Lavenham, November 21st 1644, and is one of the most important of the whole series. I shall therefore give it entire.

Right worshipful Sir,

At length my frail bark, after a difficult navigation, has safely reached the port of Lavenham. Nothing now remains for me but to return my thanks to you, under whose shadow I enjoy this happiness, and with sound principles to imbue, and with paternal care to instruct, the numerous people which you have committed to me, particularly in times like these, fermenting with many errors, when, like Rome of old, who borrowed gods from all parts of the world, we also borrow errors which have already been buried, and yet after burial again revive. My only solace in this world will now be to preserve, by earnest and continued prayer, this my congregation, pure and unspotted amongst so many corruptions.

By your letter to Henry Coppinger, I find that certain of the Sudbury people, in your hearing, have said that some new agreement had been entered into between us. I wonder from whence this fable has taken its origin. I do not admit one atom of it. It is nothing new for the sweetest wine of love sometimes to degenerate into vinegar. I hope, however, in a short time that my Sudbury friends will be restored to their former serenity, although like the troubled sea they are now in a state of considerable agitation. With respect to the Bishop, I hope he will find some other way of instituting me, or else your most honourable House will do it. And all the inhabitants of Lavenham most humbly congratulate you, right worshipful, for that in this affair you have left no stone unturned. We also earnestly desire that the matter may, if possible, be completed within these six months, which are now fast wearing away. I would willingly go to London in order that whatever remains to be done may receive the finishing stroke. May the great and good God pour His blessing on thee and thine, and may He continue to be thy sun and shield. So prays most earnestly your very humble servant in Christ, William GURNALL.

The matter referred to in the letter can, of course, only be explained by conjecture. It certainly seems to indicate that Gurnall was once a popular minister at Sudbury, and that his removal to the Rectory of Lavenham was not approved by the Sudbury people. The six months mentioned most probably mean the six months immediately following the last Rector's death. The precise date of the death of Coppinger, Gurnall's predecessor, is not known.

The sixth letter is dated Lavenham, January 6th 1645. It is clear from its contents, that whatever may have been the difficulties which stood in the way of his appointment to Lavenham, they were now all overcome, and he was finally settled in possession of the living. He says,

> Honoured Sir, most opportunely have I received the order of your honourable House. By your care and exertion alone has it been obtained; and all your favours toward me have, by this fresh proof of your kindness, been brought to a completion—this last having given perfection to the rest. What is a presentation without orders? What are orders without institution? Successfully, however, have you finished all these things so that my thanks are due to you, not only as patron, but as ordainer and institutor, for under your auspices all these things have been performed. I well know how much of your time is occupied by public business, while the arduous affairs of the nation are under consideration, and also with what indefatigable labour you pursue more severe studies. The weight therefore of this your favour is so much the more increased, when we see that among matters of greater importance you still find leisure to attend to these our affairs, trifling indeed in comparison, but such as would, I believe, from our want of skill, have been a complete snare to us, had we not been speedily delivered from them by your prudence.

About the matters referred to in this letter, we know nothing more than what Gurnall tells us. His expressions certainly seem to imply that he owed his ordination, by whatever hands he was ordained, to the interest of Sir Symond D'Ewes.

The seventh letter is dated Lavenham, March 20th 1647. It contains nothing worth quoting, and is entirely occupied with lamentations over the troublous times which the nation was passing through, and words of devout encouragement to Sir Symond D'Ewes, whose position in Parliament was probably not a very easy one at this period.

The eighth and last letter is dated October 30th 1648, and was evidently written in reply to an order of the House of Commons, calling on Gurnall to preach before the House. He says, among other things,

> Your letter reached me yesterday as I was descending from the pulpit, thoroughly fatigued; and to-day, having finished one sermon, I am preparing another for to-morrow. You will therefore, I trust, readily pardon both the brevity and unpolished style of my answer. As to the affair mentioned in your letter to me, that I have been, by an order of the House, appointed to preach before you on the 29th November next, it is a burden much too weighty for my shoulders, particularly at this time, when so many infirmities oppress me, that I can scarcely, without danger to my health, remain a short time in the open air. Much less, therefore, could I undertake so long a journey in so winterly a season. I am persuaded that the gentlemen who have proposed this know not the shattered state of my body, and have scarcely considered the distance of the place. Most humbly and earnestly, therefore, I entreat that, by your persuasion, which I know to be unparalleled, and in that honourable House most weighty, this burden may be laid on other shoulders; for, under it, in my infirm state of health, I must of necessity sink.

This letter is interesting on more than one account. It shows the high esteem in which Gurnall was held as a preacher. None but the most eminent and gifted divines of the day were summoned to preach before the House of Commons. It also shows the weak state of health in which Gurnall was at a comparatively early period of his ministry at Lavenham. To this state of health we may perhaps attribute the retired life which he seems to have lived, and the comparatively small information which we possess about him.

Having now brought Gurnall to the place where he lived and exercised his ministry for no less than thirty-five years, some information about Lavenham will probably be interesting to most readers.

Lavenham

Lavenham is a small town in the south-west corner of Suffolk, lying in a rural parish of about 2,800 acres, and containing at this time about 1,800 people. In Gurnall's time it was in the diocese of Norwich. It is now in the diocese of Ely.[58] It had once a market; and before the invention of the steam-engine, was famous for the manufacture of blue cloth and serge, for the better regulation of which three guilds, or companies, of St. Peter's, Holy Trinity, and Corpus Christi, were established. Its manufactures have now dwindled down into one silk-mill, and its market is no longer held.

The market-place, with an ancient cross in the centre, exists still. The De Veres, Earls of Oxford, were once the principal proprietors of Lavenham, and had a large park here, comprising nearly half the parish. In the reign of Elizabeth, Edward, then Earl of Oxford, sold his property at Lavenham, together with the advowson of the living, to Paul D'Ewes, Esq., father of Sir Symond D'Ewes, the patron of William Gurnall, and to this sale, therefore, the good man's connection with Lavenham must be traced.

The living to which Gurnall was appointed was, no doubt, a very valuable one. At this day the tithes are commuted at £850 a year, and there are 140 acres of glebe attached to the Rectory. Allowing for the difference in the value of money two hundred years ago, the Rector of Lavenham must have been comparatively very well off. It is, however, a curious fact, recorded by Fuller in his *Church History*, that in the year 1577 the living of Lavenham had a narrow escape of being reduced to half its value, and was only saved by the firmness of the Rector. The whole transaction is worth reading, as illustrating the disorders and irregularities in ecclesiastical matters which great laymen too often attempted to perpetrate in the

---

58 Lavenham is now in the diocese of St Edmundsbury and Ipswich. It is perhaps most famous today as the setting for parts of the final two Harry Potter films!—*Editor.*

sixteenth century, and too often with success. Fuller says,

> *In the year 1622, Henry Coppinger, formerly Fellow of St. John's College in Cambridge, Prebendary of York, once Chaplain to Ambrose, Earl of Warwick (whose funeral sermon he preached), made Master of Magdalene College, Cambridge, by his Majesty's mandates, though afterwards resigning his right at the Queen's request (shall I call it?), to prevent trouble, ended his religious life. He was the sixth son of Henry Coppinger, Esq., of Buxhall, in Suffolk, by Agnes, daughter of Sir Thomas Jermyn. His father, on his death-bed, asking him what course of life he would embrace, he answered he intended to be a divine. 'I like it well,' said the old gentleman, 'otherwise what shall I say to Martin Luther when I shall see him in heaven, and he knows that God gave me eleven sons, and I made not one of them a minister?' An expression proportionable enough to Luther's judgment, who maintained, some hours before his death, that the saints in heaven shall knowingly converse one with another.*
>
> *Lavenham living fell void, which both deserved a good minister, being a rich parsonage, and needed one, it being more than suspected that Dr. Reynolds, late Incumbent, who ran away to Rome, had left some superstitious leaven behind him. The Earl of Oxford being patron, presents Mr. Coppinger to it, but adding withal, that he would pay no tithes of his park, being almost half the land of the parish. Coppinger desired to resign it again to his lordship, rather than by such sinful gratitude to betray the rights of the Church. 'Well!' said the Earl, 'if you be of that mind, then take the tithes; I scorn that my estate should swell with Church goods.' However, it afterwards cost Mr. Coppinger sixteen hundred pounds in keeping his questioned, and recovering his detained right, in suit with the agent for the next minor Earl of Oxford and others; all which he left to his church's quiet possession, being zealous in God's cause, but remiss in his own.*
>
> *He lived forty and five years the painful parson at Lavenham, in which market-town there are about nine hundred communicants,*

> among whom, all this time, no difference did arise which he did not compound. He had a bountiful hand and plentiful purse (his paternal inheritance by death of elder brothers, and other transactions descending upon him), bequeathing twenty pounds in money, and ten pounds per annum, to the poor of the parish; in the chancel whereof he lieth buried under a fine monument, dying on St. Thomas' day, in the threescore and twelfth year of his age.

The lawsuit referred to by Fuller seems, at any rate, not to have prevented Henry Coppinger being succeeded by his son Ambrose as Rector of Lavenham, at whose death Gurnall was appointed to the living. The Henry Coppinger referred to by Gurnall in one of his letters to Sir Symond D'Ewes, was, no doubt, a member of the family of Gurnall's predecessor, and a descendant of the Rector whose firmness preserved half the tithes of Lavenham from the Earl of Oxford's shameful attempt to deprive the living of them.

Lavenham Church

The parish Church of Lavenham, in which Gurnall preached for thirty-five years, must naturally possess much interest in the eyes of all true admirers of his works. The pulpit in which the good man preached the substance of *The Christian in Complete Armour* no longer exists. But the fabric of the church is, in all probability, exactly what it was two hundred years ago.

Lavenham Church is one of the finest and handsomest ecclesiastical buildings in the county of Suffolk.

> It stands at the west end of the town, and was erected on the site of the ancient fabric, in the 15th and early part of the 16th centuries, chiefly at the cost of the Earl of Oxford, and the wealthy family of Spring, whose arms are to be seen in many parts of the building. It is in the later style of decorated English architecture, and is constructed of freestone, curiously ornamented with flint, a material commonly used in Suffolk churches, from the scarcity of stone. It is 156 feet long and 68

broad. The tower, which is of singular beauty, is 141 feet high and 42 in diameter, and contains an excellent peal of eight bells, of which the tenor weighs 23 cwt., and was cast in 1625. In the interior the roof is richly carved, and two pews, formerly belonging to the Earls of Oxford and the Springs, though now somewhat decayed, are highly finished specimens of Gothic work, in the elaborate style of Henry VII's Chapel at Westminster. In the windows are considerable remains of ancient stained glass, and the porch is of highly ornamental architecture, adorned with armorial bearings.

The above account is principally extracted from White's *History of Suffolk*, and I have no reason to doubt the accuracy of the details it contains. At the present day there can be no doubt that Lavenham is a far less important place than it was two hundred years ago. The county in which it is situated no longer occupies the position it once occupied among the counties of England. Without mines or manufactures, or large seaport towns, the eastern counties have stood still in material prosperity, while the rest of England has moved on. The village towns, with which Suffolk is rather thickly dotted, are almost all in a decaying or stationary condition. The old glory of such places as Eye, Framlingham, Bungay, Orford, Southwold, Dunwich, Aldeburgh, Hadleigh, Bildeston, Needham, Stradbroke, and Debenham, has clean passed away. Lavenham has shared the fate of these places. It is now nothing more than a quiet village in an agricultural district, remarkable only for its beautiful church and its numerous old charitable institutions.

The thirty-five years during which Gurnall lived at Lavenham, and filled the pulpit of the old parish church, were years full of stirring incidents in English history, The final overthrow of the King's party in the Commonwealth wars, the beheading of Charles I, the establishment of the Protectorate, the death of Oliver Cromwell, the restoration of the Stuarts to the throne, the passing of the Act of Uniformity, the ejection of two thousand ministers of the Church of England which followed that Act, and the intolerant persecution of all Nonconformists which disgraced this country for many years after the Act was passed, are events with which every student of English history is familiar. What Gurnall thought of most of these we have no means of knowing. What part he took, if any, and how he acted amidst the political and ecclesiastical convulsions which distracted the country we cannot say. His health in all probability prevented him from frequently leaving his own home, or doing much outside his own parish. Be the cause what it may, I am obliged to confess that the facts on record about the last thirty-five years of his life are exceedingly few.

Famous Neighbours

It is certainly somewhat remarkable that during the period of Gurnall's ministry at Lavenham, that is between 1644 and 1679, some of the best and holiest Puritan divines were at one time or another living within twenty miles of Gurnall's home at Lavenham. I will give their names.

The famous **John Owen**, whose name is familiar to every reader of pure English theology, began his ministry at Fordham and Coggeshall in Essex, and only left the latter place when Cromwell made him Dean of Christ Church in 1651 (and later Vice-Chancellor of Oxford), seven years after Gurnall became Rector of Lavenham.

Stephen Marshall, one of the most celebrated divines in the Westminster Assembly, and a prominent character in the Commonwealth times, was Minister of Wethersfield and Finchingfield in Essex, shortly before Gurnall came to Lavenham, and spent the last two years of his life at Ipswich, where he died in 1655.

Matthew Newcomen, another eminent member of the Westminster Assembly, and an assistant of Arrowsmith and Tuckney in drawing up the well-known Assembly's Catechism, was Vicar of Dedham in Essex, after the famous John Rogers was ejected in 1629, until the time of his own ejection by the Act of Uniformity, in 1662.

Thomas Young, another distinguished member of the Westminster Assembly, and Milton's tutor, was Vicar of Stowmarket in Suffolk, for the thirty years before 1643, when he became Pastor of a Church in Duke's Place, London. Afterwards, being ejected in 1650, he retired to Stowmarket, and died there in 1655. He was one of the five authors of the famous controversial work, called *Smectymnuus*, which made a great stir in the first half of the 17th century. It was so called from the initial letters of the names of its five writers: viz., Stephen Marshall, Edmund Calamy, Thomas Young, Matthew Newcomen, and William Spurstow. Of these five men, let us remember, no less than three died within a few hours' reach of Gurnall.

It would be easy to add other great names to this list, such as those of Daniel Rogers, who died at Wethersfield in 1652; Blackerby, who died at Great Thurlow in 1648; Fairclough, who was ejected from Kedington in 1662, and was succeeded by Tillotson; and Owen Stockton, who was ejected from St. Andrew's, Colchester, in 1662. Beside these good men, there were some who are less well known, such as William Sparrow of Halstead in Essex, John Fairfax of Barking in Suffolk, Matthias Candler of Coddenham in Suffolk, Samuel Spring of Creeting St. Mary in Suffolk, Stephen Scanderet of Haverhill in Suffolk, Tobias Leg of Hemingstone in Suffolk, Brunning and Stonham of Ipswich, Storer of Stowmarket—all of whom were eminent Puritan ministers, and were ejected in 1662. Their histories will be found in Calamy's *Nonconformists' Memorial*. All these men, I repeat, lived within twenty miles of Gurnall, and must have come in contact with him occasionally.

It would be deeply interesting if we knew whether Gurnall had much communication with these good men. My own private impression is that he had not. Ill-health, in all probability, kept him much at home. But I suspect this was not all. I am inclined to think that Gurnall was a man of retiring and cautious temperament, and naturally disinclined to go much into society. Above all, I am strongly inclined to think that he liked the Episcopal Church and the Prayer-book better than many of his neighbours did, and naturally withdrew from close intimacy with them. All these, however, are only conjectures, and I shall therefore pass on to the only remaining facts that remain to be told about Gurnall's history.

The Conundrum of Conformity

In the year 1645, the year following his appointment to Lavenham, Gurnall was married to Sarah Mott, daughter of the Rev. Thomas Mott, Vicar of Stoke-by-Nayland. By this lady, who survived him some years, he had ten children, eight of whom were living at his death.

In the year 1662, when no less than two thousand ministers were ejected from the Church of England by the Act of Uniformity, Gurnall signed the declaration required by the Act, on August 20th, was ordained Priest by the Bishop of Norwich, the well-known Bishop Reynolds, on August 21st, and went through the forms of Episcopal institution to Lavenham on the presentation of Thomas Bowes, of Bromley Hall, in Essex, a connection of the D'Ewes family, on August 22nd. The close proximity of these three dates is very remarkable! The result was, that while many of his Puritan brethren resigned their preferments, he retained his position as Rector of Lavenham until his death.

This part of Gurnall's history undoubtedly demands some consideration. At first sight undeniably there is something curious about it. That a minister of at least eighteen years' standing should submit to receive priest's orders at a bishop's hands, that a preacher of notoriously Puritan sentiments should sit still and retain his connection with the Church of England, while nearly all his Puritan brethren around him seceded, in all this there is something strange. That it really was so is as certain as possible. A facsimile of his subscription, which I have obtained from the Registry of Norwich, places the matter beyond doubt. It is a doubly interesting document, as containing the only specimen I know of Gurnall's hand-writing.[59]

That Gurnall's conformity brought on him great obloquy and reproach we may well suppose. A libellous attack on him was published in the year 1665, quoted by Bishop Kennett, which contains the following passage: "Neither is Mr. Gurnall alone in these horrible defilements, hateful to the Word of God and His saints, but is compassed about with a cloud

---

59 By the kindness of the Bishop of Norwich, I have been enabled to verify all the three remarkable dates above given from the Registry at Norwich.

of witnesses, even in the same county where himself liveth, men of the same order of anti-Christian priesthood and brethren in the same iniquity with himself."[60]

That he brought on himself much private sorrow and discomfort by his conformity we may easily believe. His own wife's father, Mr. Mott of Stoke-by-Nayland, was one of the two thousand who went out of the Church of England for conscience' sake. Above all, the value of his living at Lavenham, and the large size of the family dependent on him, would be sure to cause men to cast suspicion on what he did, and to question the sincerity of his motives.

But, after all, the point remains to be considered—Did Gurnall do anything inconsistent with his character as a minister of Christ? Was there anything abstractedly wrong in his conformity? Was there anything in the antecedents of his history to make it base or dishonourable to retain his post at Lavenham, to subscribe the declaration of the Act of Uniformity, to assent to the liturgy, and to submit to receive priest's orders at Bishop Reynolds' hands? On these points I have something to say.

I shall clear the way by saying that I thoroughly disapprove the Act of Uniformity, although personally I feel no difficulty about its requirements. To show my own feeling about it, I need only refer my readers to a long passage in my biography of Baxter in this volume, in which the Act of Uniformity is plainly condemned.

But while I protest against the Act of Uniformity as an unjust, unwise, impolitic, unstatesmanlike, and hard measure, I do not for a moment admit that no good man could possibly submit to its requirements. On the contrary, I can quite understand that many holy and faithful ministers

---

60 The title of this libellous attack is so curious that I give it entire. *Covenant Renouncers Desperate Apostates, opened in two letters, written by a Christian friend to Mr. W. Gurnall, of Lavenham, Suffolk, which may indefinitely serve as an admonition to all such Presbyterian ministers or others, who have forced their conscience, not only to leap over, but to renounce their solemn covenant obligation to endeavour a reformation according to God's Word, and the extirpation of all prelatical superstitions, and contrary thereunto conform to those superstitious vanities against which they had so solemnly sworn* (Printed in Anti-turn-coat Street, and sold at the sign of Truth's Delight, right opposite to Backsliding Alley. 4to, 1665).

would do as Gurnall did, and act as he acted. They would argue that we cannot have everything to our mind in this world below—that the way of patience is better than the way of secession—that there is nothing abstractedly wrong in forms of prayer—that it is better to put up with some things we do not like in a Church, than to throw away opportunities of usefulness—that it was better to accept the Prayer-book with all its blemishes, and have liberty to preach the gospel, than to refuse the Prayer-book and be silenced altogether—that so long as the *Thirty-nine Articles* were sound and uninjured, they could not be compelled to preach unsound doctrine—and that so long as they were allowed to preach sound doctrine, they ought not to refuse the opportunity, but to preach, and stand by their flocks. All this I can conceive a good man saying to himself. Whether Gurnall reasoned in this manner I cannot pretend to say. But I think he might have done so.

The plain truth is, that before any one condemns Gurnall for submitting to the Act of Uniformity, he ought in common justice to remember the times and circumstances in which Gurnall first entered the ministry. He became a minister of the gospel at a period in English history when it was impossible to obtain Episcopal ordination, and the use of the Prayer-book was almost forbidden. I have no doubt he was quite right in accepting the position of things which he found around him. The imposition of Episcopal hands is not absolutely necessary to make a valid ordination. The use of the Church of England liturgy is not essential to the being of a Church. At the time when Gurnall entered the ministry he could neither have Episcopacy nor the Prayer-book, and he entered the ministry without them. Let others say what they will, I do not think he was wrong. It is better to have the gospel preached without Bishops and Prayer-books, than not to have any preaching at all.

But, after all, there is not the slightest proof that Gurnall had any conscientious objection either to Episcopacy or the liturgy of the Church of England. For anything we can discover, he had never committed himself to any such condemnation of them as to make it inconsistent to approve and adopt them. What right, then, have we to find fault with him because he submitted to the requirements of the Act of 1662? He was ordained priest by Bishop Reynolds, because he could not be an Incumbent in the diocese without priest's orders. But who shall say that he would not gladly have received Episcopal orders twenty years before, if it had been possible to obtain them? He declared his assent and consent to all things contained in the Prayer-book. But who shall say that he would not have done the same at any period in his life? He had never been a member of the Westminster Assembly, like many of the two thousand ejected divines. He had never been mixed up in their public proceedings, discussions, and controversies like Owen, Newcomen, Baxter, and many more. He had been a quiet, retired preacher in a country parish, and there is really no proof whatever that his retention of his position at Lavenham was inconsistent with anything in his previous life.

One more circumstance ought not to be forgotten in forming our estimate of Gurnall's conduct at this crisis of his life. The Bishop in whose diocese he was living, and at whose hands he accepted re-ordination, was Bishop Reynolds, himself a Puritan in doctrine, and notoriously the most mild and lenient man on the Episcopal bench in dealing with scrupulous clergymen. We cannot doubt that such a man as Reynolds would use every effort to meet Gurnall's scruples, if he had any. We cannot doubt that he would strain every nerve to retain as many of the clergy as possible within the pale of the Church, and to prevent secessions.

I confess to a strong suspicion that this circumstance weighed much in Gurnall's mind. Few men can do more by kindness, and less by harshness, in dealing with men, than bishops. If Gurnall ever had any doubts about remaining in the Church of England, in 1662, I think it very likely that his good Bishop's character turned the scale. In short, I venture the guess, that he might have gone out of Lavenham Rectory, and followed his father-in-law, Mr. Mott, in secession, if the occupier of Norwich palace had been any other bishop than Reynolds.[61]

---

61 Reynolds was made Bishop of Norwich by Charles II in 1661. He was a thorough Puritan and a prominent member of the famous Westminster Assembly of Divines. When the Bishopric of Norwich was offered to him, the Bishopric of Hereford at the same time was offered to

I leave the subject of Gurnall's conduct in 1662 with the reader. It is one on which different men will have different opinions, according to the standpoint which they occupy. Some in the present day would have thought more highly of Gurnall if he had refused to submit to the Act of Uniformity, and had gone out with the famous two thousand. I, and many others perhaps, think more highly of him because he held his ground and did not secede. Which of us is right will never, probably, be settled in this world. I only desire to record my own opinion, that Gurnall was probably just as courageous, conscientious, and high-principled in deciding to stay in, as hundreds of his two thousand ejected brethren were in deciding to go out. In movements like that of 1662, the seceding party has not always a monopoly of grace and courage. There were many cases, I have no doubt, in which it showed more courage to submit to the Act of Uniformity than to refuse submission, and in which it cost a man far more to hold his living than to throw it up. I should not wonder if Gurnall's was one.

About Gurnall's life after the year 1662 we know literally nothing at all. We may well suppose that his latter years were saddened by the events of the year 1662. Human nature would not be what it is, if his retention of his position, and subscription to the Act of Uniformity, did not create some estrangement of feeling between himself and his seceding brethren. But we really have no right to speak decidedly on the matter. There are floating traditions in the neighbourhood of Lavenham that he never was the same man as a minister after 1662, that he had been before; that there was no power or blessing attending his ministry from that time forward. But I must plainly say, that I cannot discover any foundation for these traditions. I regard them as nothing better than lying stories. Such stories are often current about eminent servants of Christ.

Baxter, the Bishopric of Lichfield to Calamy, the Deanery of Rochester to Manton, and the Deanery of Coventry to Bates. All these eminent Puritan divines refused preferment when Reynolds accepted it. Their refusal, I venture to think, was the greatest misfortune that ever befell the Church of England, and the most singular instance of mistaken judgment on record in Church history. If Reynolds, Baxter, and Calamy had all been bishops, and sat in the House of Lords, and Manton and Bates had been deans, I doubt if the Act of Uniformity, in its present shape, could ever have been passed.

His refusal to give up his post at Lavenham, when many other ministers seceded, would, no doubt, give great annoyance to the bitterest and most extreme Nonconformists in that part of Suffolk, since it would weaken their hands and strengthen the Church of England. I should therefore expect, as a matter of course, that all manner of false reports would be current about him. Lies are Satan's chief weapons against God's saints.

Gurnall's Death and Funeral

Gurnall died, October 12th 1679, and was buried at Lavenham, in the sixty-third year of his age. There is internal evidence, we have already seen, in his letters and elsewhere, that he was always a man of weak health. But we know not whether he died suddenly or of a lingering illness. The fact, however, that he made his will the day before he died would rather point to the conclusion that he had been ill some time.

M'Keon, to whose biography of Gurnall I have so frequently referred, has procured a copy of Gurnall's will, which I here subjoin, as it may interest many readers.—

> *In the name of God, Amen. The Eleventh day of October, in the year of our Lord, One Thousand Six Hundred and Seventy-nine, I, William Gurnall of Lavenham, in the county of Suffolk, clerk, weak of body, but, thanks be to God, of sound mind and memory, resigning up my soul in the first place into the hands of God, my Lord, Redeemer, and Saviour, and yielding my body to the earth, to be buried at the discretion of my executrix, as concerning that worldly estate which it has pleased God to bestow upon me, do make and ordain, this, my last will and testament as followeth:*
>
> *That is to say, I give and decree all my free land and tenements, with all their appurtenances whatsoever, lying and being in Walpole or elsewhere, in Monkland, in the county of Norfolk, unto Sarah, my well-beloved wife and her heirs, to hold to her, the said Sarah, to her own proper use, for, and during the time of her natural life, and after her decease to some one of my children, as she shall declare in, and*

by her last will and testament. And I do give and decree also all my goods and chattels, debts, and personal estate whatsoever, unto the said Sarah, my well-beloved wife, as well for her own comfortable subsistence and maintenance, and the better to enable her for the bringing up of my younger children, as also in trust and confidence that she will preserve and dispose of the residue and surplusage thereof amongst my children, respecting the circumstances of those of them which are not yet provided for, in such manner, and in such proportion as in her discretion she shall think most meet and fit; only I decree, if my son John shall be a scholar, that she will give my books to him. And I do hereby nominate, constitute, and appoint the said Sarah, my well-beloved wife, to be sole executrix of this my will, which I have caused to be written and have thereunto set my hand and seal, the day of grace aforesaid.

Subscribed, sealed, published, and declared by the said William Gurnall, to be his last will and testament, in the presence of us, Thomas Mott, Bezaleel Peachie, John Pinchbeck.

The first of these three witnesses was most probably the father or brother of Mrs. Gurnall. She was daughter of Thomas Mott. The second was evidently the husband of his third daughter, Catherine. The third was perhaps the lawyer who drew up the will. The books mentioned in the will are probably the very books which Gurnall's son, John, afterwards left by his will, in 1699, to his brother Joseph, and his nephew Leonard Shaftoe of Newcastle. The English books were left to Joseph Gurnall, and the "rest of the books and manuscripts" to Leonard Shaftoe. They are now probably scattered to the four winds, and dispersed, if not destroyed. The end to which good men's libraries finally come is a melancholy subject. Few things are so much loved by some, and despised and neglected by others as books, and specially theological books.

The precise spot in which Gurnall was buried is not known. We cannot tell whether his bones are lying in the Church or in the churchyard. No tombstone or monumental slab marks the place of his interment.

Nothing, from some cause or other, seems to have been erected to his memory. "The only sepulchral notice to be found of him," says M'Keon, "is on a black marble slab in the chancel, which has this inscription:

> 'Here lieth the body of Mary, late wife of Mr. Henry Boughton, of this parish, and daughter of the late Reverend Mr. Samuel Beachcroft, Rector of Semer, and granddaughter of the late Reverend Mr. William Gurnall, who was Rector of this parish thirty-five years. She died the 14th of October, 1741, aged 78 years.'"

Under this slab in the chancel is a vault, which M'Keon conjectured is Gurnall's resting-place, from the fact of Mrs. Boughton having been buried here instead of being buried with the Boughton family in the family vault, near the great south door. However, it is only a conjecture.

A funeral sermon was preached in Lavenham Church, in commemoration of Gurnall, shortly after his funeral, by the well-known commentator on the New Testament, Burkitt, who was at that time Rector of Milden, near Lavenham. It is still extant, and bears the following title: *The people's zeal provoked to an holy emulation by the pious and instructive example of their dead Minister; as a seasonable memento to the parishioners of Lavenham in Suffolk.*

Burkitt's sermon was on Hebrews 13:7, "Remember them that have the rule over you," etc. It was both preached and published "by request," and is prefaced by an epistle dedicatory "to my honoured friend, Mrs. Sarah Gurnall, the sorrowful relict of Mr. William Gurnall, late of Lavenham, deceased, and to the rest of the sorrowing inhabitants of that town." It is a respectable composition, though somewhat quaint, and rather flowery and highflown in style. But it is but fair to Burkitt to remember that he was comparatively young when he preached it, being only twenty-nine years old. A few extracts from it will probably be found interesting. I shall select those parts only which refer to Gurnall.

Burkitt's epistle dedicatory concludes with the following passage:

> *To inform and convince you how highly accountable you are to Al-*

mighty God, both for the long enjoyment of his ministry, and also for the happy advantage of his example, is the honest design of the following sermon; and also to let this censorious age (in which some persons are so overgrown with the anti-episcopal jaundice, that their eye can see nothing in a Conformist but what is discoloured and of a different tincture), understand and know that you had a Conformist for your minister, who rendered solid religion amiable, by a conversation in all things worthy of it; who did by a regular piety, a strict sobriety, a catholic and diffusive charity, render religion venerable to the world; one whose whole time, strength, and parts, were piously devoted to God and His sacred service.

Moses, I observe, was in one particular privileged by God above all other holy persons. Their souls (in common with his) at death have angels for their convoy towards the mansions of bliss and glory: but he had an angel for his sexton, who buried his body in an unknown place, lest the Israelites should superstitiously idolize and adore it. There would be no fear at all of any such offensive adoration on your part, were I able (as indeed I am not) to draw to the life the fair effigies of your absent minister, who was, like Moses, faithful in all God's house whilst he lived, and not unlike him at his death: his meek soul gliding from him in a fine, imperceptible vehicle; and he dying as the modern Jews by tradition tell us Moses did, **ad nutum Dei, et osculo oris ejus**,—*at God's beck, and as it were with a kiss of God's mouth. It was no more betwixt God and them but this,—Go up and die.*

To conclude, then, may all your practices appear to the world in a faithful compliance with what was truly imitable and praise-worthy in him. May the living example of your dead minister be exemplified in the lives of you his people. May you daily dress by his glass, and walk in his pious and devout footsteps. May you all meet him with astonishing joy, and behold him also with unutterable delight and comfort, in the day of your great audit: this is, and ever shall be, the hearty and affectionate supplication of your sympathising friend and servant,

William Burkitt.

Milden, Dec. 10, 1679.

The sermon contains the following sentences which are worth transcribing: "How lovely was that copy of religion which he set before you in his daily conversation! So forcible was the majesty of that holiness that shined forth in him, that it did extort a veneration from its most violent opposers; and so convictive also that it pierced the very consciences of his enemies, and constrained them whom prejudice only had made his foes, tacitly to acknowledge that God was in him of a truth."[62]

Again: "He being dead, yet speaketh: yea, dead as well as living, he is still your preacher, his shroud and coffin are his pulpit—his grave and tombstone are his temple, and he still preaches to you though he lies in silence before you and utters never a word; I mean by his pious and most instructive example left among you, and by that fair character and good report which he hath so deservedly obtained with you."[63]

Again: "I am sure it did not a little conduce to the Support of your dying Minister's spirit, when he had death before him in immediate prospect, to hope upon good grounds that he (as a spiritual father) should leave many children behind him, to carry on the work of Christ in the world, when his head should be laid among the clods."[64]

The last five pages of the sermon are so entirely occupied with Gurnall's character, that I think it best to give them unabridged:

> *I infer from hence, in the last place, how signal your obligations are to Almighty God for the long enjoyment of that exemplary pattern of all true piety and virtue (your deceased Minister, I mean), whom (for your sins, I fear) He hath lately taken from you. Show now your obedience to God, your respects to him, your kindness and charity to your own souls, by a zealous and faithful care to transcribe impartially in your own lives whatever was truly imitable in your Minister's. And not to carry you beyond the confines of the text, let me earnestly be-*

---

62 Page 9 (Baynes' reprint, 1829).

63 Pages 10-11.

64 Page 17.

speak your Christian compliance with a double duty here enjoined.

I. To follow his faith.

II. To imitate his exemplary conversation.

III. Follow his faith, and that in a double respect, in the soundness of his faith, and in the steadfastness of his faith.

1. Follow him in the soundness of his faith. *The faith which he perseveringly professed, and taught, was that doctrine which is according to godliness; that faith which owns God for its immediate Author and the Scripture for its infallible rule, the faith that was once delivered to the saints, which is not the result of fancy and imagination, but the product of an eternal counsel, which was confirmed by the miracles and sealed with the blood of a Saviour. In a word, that faith which he so zealously taught had sure footing in the Holy Scriptures. Whenever he propounded any truth which required not only the assent of your understandings, but also the obedience and adoration of your faith, he constantly showed you the Canon of the Scriptures for its confirmation. If any then (which God forbid) should appear after him in this place, and attempt the proselyting of you to another Gospel, or to any new doctrine of faith foreign to the Scriptures, should he pretend to the authority of a commissioned angel from heaven, let him be held accursed.*

2. Follow him in the steadfastness of his faith. *The same rule of faith which he laid before you at his first coming amongst you, he lived and preached by till the day of his death. And this I take the greater liberty to assert, because some persons have not blushed to tell the world publicly that since his conformity to the discipline of the Church he had apostatized and revolted from that faith which he had formerly professed and taught. But be ye all assured, that, as to the great fundamentals of faith and religion, he was ever the same, and what he taught you to his last breath, I doubt not but he stood ready to confirm and seal with his blood, even in the fiercest flames of martyrdom, if God had called him to that fiery trial.*

II. Imitate his Christian conversation. My meaning is, exemplify those Evangelical graces and Christian virtues in your lives, which did so oriently shine forth in his. To propound a few:—

1. His eminent humility. This was the garment which covered all his excellent accomplishments, although indeed their beauty was rendered more conspicuous and amiable by casting this veil over it. O what mean thoughts had he of himself! and was not only content but desirous also, that others should have so too: no man ever expressed so low a value of his worth and merits as himself did. Everything in others that was good he admired as excellent, whilst the same or better in himself he thought not unworthily contemned: his eyes were full of his own deficiencies and others' perfections.

In a word, he was a lovely valley, sweetly planted, well watered, richly fruitful: imitate him then herein, and by a holy emulation study to excel him in this adorning grace; and for your help herein recollect what you heard from him in his elaborate discourses among you upon Phil. ii. 5: 'Let this mind be in you, which was also in Christ Jesus,'—this humble mind.

2. His extensive love. This grace did variously exert itself.

(1) His love to God. He loved Him exceedingly whom he could not love excessively, having such high and raised apprehensions of his Maker's excellencies, as caused him to judge his prime and best affections unworthy to be placed on so Divine an object.

(2) His love to the holy Jesus. This was such a seraphic and Divine fire in his soul, as did marvellously consume his love to the world and all sublunary comforts. You are witnesses, and all that knew him, in how eminent a measure and degree the world was crucified unto him, and he unto the world by the cross of Christ.

(3) His love to souls. This was it, no doubt, that made him so indefatigable both in his study and in the pulpit; from hence it was, that the throne of grace, his study, the pulpit, and his sick neighbours, had the *whole of his time divided amongst them, and devoted to them.*

(4) His Unbounded Love To All Christians; *though they differed in their sentiments from him. He loved Christians for their Christianity, and did adore the image of his Saviour wherein he saw it in any of his members unhappily persecuting one another with hard names and characters of reproach. How often did he Publicly Deplore And Bewail, that the greatest measure of love that is found at this day amongst the professors of the cross, was not true Christian love, but only love of a party! Follow him, then, in the impartial exercise of this grace, and for your help therein remember what he taught you from Ephesians 5:2, 'And walk in love, as Christ also hath loved us;' and as you have any regard for the Author of your profession, take heed that a spirit of division (now) crowd not in among you. Your unity is your strength as well as your beauty; persist therefore, I beseech you, in that Christian order amongst yourselves in which it was his great ambition all his days to preserve and keep you. Timely oppose the crafty design of the subtle adversary of souls, who will take this occasion (if possible), now the spiritual parent is out of the way, to set the children together by the ears.*

3. His diffusive charity. *His alms were as exuberant as his love: misery and want, wherever he met them, did sufficiently endear their objects to him. He was none of those that hide their faces from the poor, nor of the number of them who satisfy their consciences with a single exercise of their charity once a year, but daily were the emanations of his bounty. Yet although he cast the seeds of his charity upon all sorts of ground, he sowed them thickest upon God's inclosure: my meaning is, he did good unto all, but especially to those that were of the household of faith.' Make him herein, and his example, the pattern of your daily imitation; for the world, which is chained together by intermingled love, will soon shatter and fall in pieces if charity shall once fail and die; and for your better help herein, call over those potent arguments for the exercise of this Evangelical duty, which he urged upon you, from that apostolical injunction, Hebrews 13:16, 'But to do good, and to communicate, forget not, for with such sacrifices God* is well pleased.'

4. His persevering diligence and faithfulness in his place and station. You could not but observe that his whole disposal of himself was to perpetual industry and service. He not only avoided idleness, but seemed to have a forcible antipathy against it, and was often recommending it to you with great concern and vigour in his public advices, to be always furnished with somewhat to do; *ut te inveniat semper diabolus occupatum*: that the devil may never find thee at leisure to listen to his temptations, as St. Jerome adviseth. The idle man's brain being, in truth, not only the devil's shop, but his kingdom too, a model of and an appendage unto hell; a place (like that) given up to torture and mischief. As to himself, his chiefest recreation was variety of work; for beside those portions of time which the necessities of nature and of civil life extorted from him, there was not a minute of the day which he left vacant. Now to stimulate your zeal to a pious imitation of him herein also, let me admonish you to ruminate upon those accurate sermons you heard from him upon Matthew 20:6: 'Why stand ye here all the day idle?'

5. His tender sympathy with the afflicted Church of Christ. Like a true son of Zion, he could not rejoice when his mother mourned, he daily felt as much by sympathy as he did by sense; and no wonder, for he that hath a stock going in the Church's ship, cannot but lament and quake at every storm. O how frequent were his inquiries after her, how fervent were his prayers for her, how bowelly and compassionate were his mournings over her! The deplorable condition of the Church and nation lay exceeding near his heart both living and dying; he preferring their happiness and welfare above his chief joy. Now in order to your attaining the same Christ-like temper with him, frequently meditate on what you heard from him upon Nehemiah 1:4, where the sympathising prophet refuseth to drink wine, when the afflicted Church drank water.

6. And lastly, to sum up all, imitate him in his daily care and

endeavour to live religion in all his capacities. As a minister, ye are witnesses, and God also, how faithfully, how conscientiously he discharged his duty towards you. In the exercise of his ministerial function, if censure itself be able to tax him for any neglect, it must be in not more frequent visiting his flock, from which nothing but a weak body kept him, not a proud or unwilling mind. The obstruction he met with in this part of his duty, from his tender habit of body (which would not suffer him so frequently to perform it as he desired) was his great sorrow both living and dying; yet having this to comfort him, that the frailty of his body was his affliction, but not his sin.

Consider him in his next relative capacity, as a child, how dutiful and obsequious! O how great was that tribute of veneration and respect which he so constantly paid to the hoary hairs of his aged parents! As a husband, how tender and compassionate; as a parent, how indulgent and affectionate; as a minister, how kind and munificent! Thus was he universally good in all stations, and lived religion in every capacity. And if you desire to imitate him herein also, as becomes you, dress your souls by that glass daily, which his dying hand last held up before your eyes: I mean by heavenly meditation, make those useful truths your own, which you last heard from him upon Titus 2:12, 'That, denying ungodliness and worldly lusts, we should live soberly, righteously, and godly in this present world.' Which Christian lesson, if it shall be as practically learned by you as it was faithfully taught by him, I will be bold to say thus much in the singular commendation of you his people, that you will thereby give the world a convictive instance that this age hath virtues as stupendous as its vices!

The Conclusion—Thus I have given myself the satisfaction of doing my duty in propounding your Minister's example to your Christian view. Let none censoriously say I have been all this while painting the prophet's sepulchre. No, but describing the prophet himself, and with this single and sincere intention, that you may timely know you have had a prophet of the Lord among you; a person that had *omnia in se sempiterna præter corpusculum:* all things living and lasting to *eternity except his body, which was the only thing he had subject to mortality, and besides which nothing of him doth see corruption. It will be below the merit of his person, as well as the greatness of our loss, to celebrate his death in womanish complaints, or indeed by any verbal lamentations; nor can anything beseem his memory but what is sacred and Divine, as his writings are. May his just fame from them, and from his virtues, be precious to all succeeding ages. And when elegies committed to the trust of marble shall be as illegible as if they had been writ in water, when all stately pyramids shall be dissolved in dust, and all the venerable monuments of antiquity be devoured by the corroding teeth of time, then let this short character, describing him in his best and fullest portraiture, remain of him: viz., that he was a* **Christian In Complete Armour.**

Circumstances at Lavenham, we can easily see, are referred to in this funeral sermon, of which we know nothing certain now. It is evident that Gurnall's troubles during the latter part of his incumbency were neither few nor small. His conformity in 1662 was probably never forgotten; and the last years of his life were probably darkened by the implacable enmity of some of his parishioners. That Burkitt, who doubtless knew more of Gurnall's inner life than any one, should have given the world no biography of him, is much to be regretted. He could have done it well, and it is a pity that he did not do it.

Gurnall's widow survived her husband nineteen years, and seems to have resided at Lavenham. At any rate, she was buried at Lavenham on September 7th 1698, and the grant of administration to her property called her "Sarah Gurnall, widow, of Lavenham, deceased."

Gurnall left at least eight children, according to M'Keon, two having died young:

1. **Sarah**, baptized April 2nd 1646, married to Mr. Mayor, of Newcastle-on-Tyne.

2. **Susannah**, baptized April 4th 1650, married the Rev. Samuel Beachcroft, of Emmanuel College, Cambridge, Rector of Semer,

Suffolk.

3. **Catherine**, the date of whose baptism we do not know, married the Rev. Bezaleel Peachie, of Emmanuel College, Cambridge, Vicar of Bures St. Mary, near Sudbury, who was one of the witnesses of Gurnall's will.

4. **Elizabeth**, baptized April 25th 1655, married the Rev. Philip Richardson, of Christ's College, Cambridge, a clergyman of Ipswich.

5. **Ann**, baptized February 11th 1655, continued to live with her mother at Lavenham until her decease in 1698, and married in June 1700, Mr. William Manthorpe of Lowestoft.

6. **Another sister**, whose name is not known, married a Mr. Shaftoe, of Newcastle-on-Tyne.

7. **Thomas**, baptized March 13th 1659, settled at Little Waldringfield, and was buried there in 1723.

8. **Joseph**, baptized July 23rd 1662, was an attorney, and according to M'Keon's belief, resided at Lavenham.

9. **John**, baptized December 24th 1664, was sent to Christ's College, proceeded B.A. in 1685, and afterwards became Curate of Brockley, until 1698. He was buried at Lavenham on February 6th 1700.

10. **Leonard**, baptized May 11th 1669, is one of whom nothing is known.

I can find no trace of Gurnall's descendants in the present day. There is no one, so far as I can learn, of his name at Lavenham. The Rectory House in which he lived is no longer standing. The living of Lavenham has passed into the hands of Caius College, Cambridge. Everything connected with the good man, except his book, seems to have passed away. By it alone, "he being dead yet speaketh" (Hebrews 11:4).

I have now completely exhausted all the information I can supply about the author of *The Christian in Complete Armour*, and can only express my deep regret that I can tell the reader nothing more. It certainly does seem rather tantalizing that a writer of the seventeenth century who is better known by name than almost any of the Puritans, who lived within twenty miles of such men as Owen, Marshall, Newcomen, Young, and Stockton, who resided for thirty-five years in a town of some little importance two hundred years ago, in a county so well known at that time as Suffolk—that such a man should have passed away and so very little be known about him! But so it is. Gurnall's case, perhaps, does not stand alone. Perhaps the last day will prove that some of the best and holiest men that ever lived are hardly known.

Gurnall's Writings

Nothing now remains for me to do except to say a few words about Gurnall's literary works, which have been lately, for the first time, brought together in a complete form.[65]

The first of Gurnall's works, and indeed the one by which he is commonly known, is his famous book, *The Christian in Complete Armour*. This well-known book consists, like many of the theological writings of the seventeenth century, of sermons or lectures delivered by the author in the course of his regular ministry, in a consecutive course, on Ephesians 6:10-20.

It was originally published in three small quarto volumes, and in three portions, at three different times. The first volume, containing Ephesians 6:10-13, was published in 1655. This volume is dedicated to "the Inhabitants of Lavenham, my dearly beloved friends and neighbours", and the dedication contains a distinct statement, that the book consists of sermons preached at Lavenham. "What I present you," says Gurnall, "within this treatise, is a dish from your own table, and so (I hope) will go down the better. You cannot despise it, though the fare be mean, except you will blame yourselves who chose the cook." There is

---

[65] I refer to Blackie's complete edition of Gurnall's works, which I take the opportunity of strongly recommending to all buyers of theology.

a date at the end of the dedication which happily serves to show when the work was published. It is dated January 1st 1655. My copy is the second edition.

The second volume of the course, containing Ephesians 6:14-16 was published in 1658. It contains a dedication to "Thomas Darcy, Esq., and Mrs. Sisilia Darcy, his religious consort," at Kentwell Hall in Suffolk; from which it appears that Mrs. Darcy was daughter of Sir Symond D'Ewes, Gurnall's patron. The dedication is dated Lavenham, October 1657. My copy is the first edition.

The third volume of the. work, containing Ephesians 6:17-20 was published in 1662. It is dedicated to Lady Mary Vere, Baroness of Tilbury; a lady well known in the seventeenth century, and daughter of William Tracey, Esq., of Toddington in Gloucestershire. The dedication is dated August 28th 1661. My copy is the first edition.

Comment, or recommendation, is perhaps needless in speaking of Gurnall's great work. The fact that a sixth edition was published in the year the author died, 1679, is enough to show that its merits were early recognised. The high reputation it has always borne among lovers of sound English divinity down to the present day, is another fact which ought not to be forgotten. Other theological works of the seventeenth century were famous in their day, but are now seldom read. *The Christian in Complete Armour* is a work that is read and enjoyed by thousands up to this time.

One grand peculiarity of *The Christian in Complete Armour* is the soundness and Scriptural proportion of its doctrinal statements. There is nothing extravagant and overstretched in Gurnall's exhibition of any point, either in faith or practice. Nothing is glaringly over-coloured, nothing is completely thrown into the shade. In this respect it is eminently like Bunyan's *Pilgrim's Progress*, a work so beautifully proportioned in doctrine, that Calvinists and Arminians, Churchmen and Dissenters, are all alike agreed in admiring it.

Another striking peculiarity of Gurnall's book is its profusion of illustrations and comparisons. You can hardly open a page of the work without meeting with some vivid image or picture of Divine things, which lights up the whole subject under consideration like a sunbeam. I am not prepared to say that in this respect Gurnall surpasses Brooks, Watson, or Swinnock, but I am quite sure that he deserves to be classed with them. Happy would it be for the Church if this gift of illustration was more common and more cultivated by preachers! The man whose sermons are best remembered is the man who, like his Divine Master, "uses similitudes." "He is the eloquent man," says an Oriental proverb, "who turns his hearers' ears into eyes, and makes them see what he speaks of."

One more beautiful feature in Gurnall's book is its richness in pithy, pointed, and epigrammatical sayings. Page after page might be filled, if a collection were made of all the short, golden sentences which are to be found in *The Christian in Complete Armour*. You will often find in a line and a half some great truth, put so concisely, and yet so fully, that you really marvel how so much thought could be got into so few words.

It would be easy to heap up testimonies to the value of Gurnall's *Christian in Complete Armour*. Baxter and Flavel both thought most highly of the book. Toplady used to make copious extracts from it in his commonplace book. John Newton said that if he was confined to one book beside the Bible, he dared say Gurnall's *Christian Armour* would be his choice. Cecil spent many of the last days of his life in reading it, and repeatedly expressed his admiration of it. But I have said enough already to weary the reader, and the best advice I can give him is to read the book for himself in the beautiful edition in which it has lately been brought out by Messrs. Blackie, and to judge for himself.[66]

Two other books, and two only, are known to have been published by Gurnall, in addition to his great work, *The Christian in Complete Armour*. Both of these are single sermons preached on special occasions.

One of these sermons is called *The Magistrate's Portraiture drawn from*

---

[66] More recently, the Banner of Truth have produced a three-volume modernised abridgement of the work— *Editor*.

the Word. It was preached at Stowmarket in Suffolk, upon August 20th 1656, "before the election of Parliament recurs for the same county," and published the same year. The subject of the sermon is Isaiah 1:26. It is an excellent sermon, and worthy of the author in every way.

The other sermon is called *The Christian's Labour and Reward*. It was preached at Castle Hedingham in Essex, on January 10th 1671, and published in 1672. It consists chiefly of a discourse preached at the funeral of Lady Mary Vere, widow of Sir Horace Vere of Tilbury; the lady to whom the third volume of *The Christian in Complete Armour* is dedicated. It contains a dedication to Elizabeth, Countess Dowager of Clare, who was Lady Mary Vere's daughter. It is a good sermon, undoubtedly, but would have been better if it had been more compressed. However, the preachers of funeral sermons are seldom allowed much time for their preparation, and perhaps Gurnall had no time to make his sermon shorter.

I have seen it asserted that Gurnall, in addition to the works already mentioned, published a volume of sermons in 1660. M'Keon says that this volume is mentioned in Cooke's *Preacher's Assistant*, published in 1783, and that a bookseller in London told him that he had himself seen a copy.

In reply to this I can only say that no such volume of sermons is to be found in the British Museum, nor in the Bodleian Library at Oxford, nor in the Redcross Street Library in London. Neither can I hear of any living man, whether bookseller or collector of old divinity, who ever saw the volume. I must therefore be allowed to think that M'Keon made a mistake, and that no such volume was ever published.

I now conclude this lengthy biography by expressing my earnest hope that Gurnall's works may yet find many readers as well as purchasers. It is indeed to be desired that solid, Scriptural theology, like that contained in *The Christian in Complete Armour*, should be valued and studied in the Church. Books in which Scripture is reverently regarded as the only rule of faith and practice, books in which Christ and the Holy Ghost have their rightful office, books in which justification, and sanctification, and regeneration, and faith, and grace, and holiness are clearly, distinctly, and accurately delineated, and exhibited—these are the only books which do real good. Few things need reviving more than a taste for such books as these among readers.

For my own part, I can only say that I read everything I can get hold of which professes to throw light on my Master's business, and the work of Christ among men. But the more I read, the less I admire modern theology. The more I study the productions of the new schools of theological teachers, the more I marvel that men and women can be satisfied with such writing. There is a vagueness, a mistiness, a shallowness, an indistinctness, a superficiality, an aimlessness, a hollowness about the literature of the Catholic or broader systems, as they are called, which, to my mind, stamps their origin on their face. They are of the earth, earthy. I find more of definite soul-satisfying thought in one page of Gurnall than in five pages of such books as the leaders of the so-called "Catholic" and "Broad Church Schools" put forth. In matters of theology "the old is better."

5. James II and the Seven Bishops

The reign of James II is a period of English history which has left a greater mark on this country than any period since the Reformation. It is a period to which we owe our civil and religious liberties, and the maintenance of our Protestantism, and as such it deserves the attention of every true-hearted Englishman. I propose in this chapter to give a general sketch of the leading events in the reign of James II, and a more particular account of the famous trial of the Seven Bishops. If the whole subject does not throw broad, clear light on our position and duties in the present day, I am greatly mistaken.

The reign of James II was a singularly short one. It began in February 1685 and ended in December 1688. Short as his reign was, it is no exaggeration to say that it contains a more disgraceful list of cruel, stupid, unjust, and tyrannical actions, for which the Sovereign alone can be held responsible, than the reign of any constitutional monarch of this land, with the single exception of Bloody Mary. It is a reign, in fact, in our English annals without one redeeming feature. Not one grand victory stirs our patriotic feelings; not one first-class statesman or general, and hardly a bishop beside Ken and Pearson, rouses our admiration; and the majestic name of Sir Isaac Newton among men of science stands almost alone. There were few giants in the land. It was an era of mediocrity; it was an age not of gold, or silver, or brass, or iron, but of lead. We turn away from the picture with shame and disgust, and it abides in our memories as a picture in which there is no light and all shade.

The chief explanation of this singularly disgraceful reign is to be found in the fact that James II was a narrow-minded, obstinate, zealous, thorough-going member of the Church of Rome. As soon as he ascended the throne he surrounded himself with priests and Popish advisers, and placed confidence in none but Papists. Within a month of his accession, says Evelyn in his diary, "the Romanists were swarming at Court with greater confidence than had ever been seen in England since the Reformation."[67] At his coronation he refused to receive the Sacrament according to the rites of the Church of England. He set up a Popish chapel at his Court, and attended Mass.

He strained every nerve throughout his reign to encourage the spread of Popery and discourage Protestantism. He procured the visit of a Popish nuncio, and demeaned himself before him as no English sovereign ever did since the days of King John. He told Barillon, the French Ambassador, that his first object was to obtain for the Romanists the free exercise of their religion, and then at last to give them absolute supremacy.[68] All this was done in a country which, little more than a century before, had been freed from Popery by the martyred Reformers, and blessed with organized Protestantism by the reign of Elizabeth. Can any one wonder that the God of Providence was displeased, and refused to show the light of his countenance on the land? James II's reign was an unhappy and discreditable time in the annals of England, because the King was a thorough-going Papist.

The second explanation of the disgraceful character of James II's times is to be found in the low moral condition of the whole nation when he came to the throne. The mis-government of James I and Charles I, the semi-Popish proceedings of Archbishop Laud, the fierce civil war of the Commonwealth, the iron rule of Oliver Cromwell, the rebound into

---

67 Knight, *History of England*, volume 4, page 383.

68 If any one doubts this, I refer him to the histories of England by Hallam (volume 3, page 73), Ranke (volume 4, pages 216, 218, 219), and Stoughton (volume 2, page 108).

unbridled licentiousness which attended the Restoration and reign of Charles II, the miserably unwise and unjust Act of Uniformity, the unceasing persecution of true religion under the pretence of doing God service and making men of one mind—all these things had borne their natural fruit. The England of James II's time was morally vile and rotten to the core.

The Court seems to have thrown aside common decency, and to have regarded adultery and fornication as no sin at all. Evelyn's description of what he saw at Whitehall the very week that Charles II died is sad and disgusting. On Sunday evening, the 1st of February 1685, Evelyn, it seems, was at Whitehall. A week after he recorded his impressions of the scene which he then witnessed: "I can never forget the inexpressible luxury and profaneness, and, as it were, total forgetfulness of God, it being Sunday evening. The King sitting and toying with his concubines, Portsmouth, Cleveland, Mazarin, etc.: a French boy singing love songs in that glorious gallery; whilst above twenty of the great courtiers and other dissolute persons were at Basset around a large table, a bank of at least two thousand in gold before them." On Monday morning, the 2nd of February, the King was struck with apoplexy.

Charles Knight (in his *History of England*) truly says:

> *The high public spirit, the true sense of honour, which had characterized the nobles and gentry of England during the Civil War, was lost in the selfishness, the meanness, the profligacy, of the twenty-eight years that succeeded the Restoration. Traitors were hatched in the sunshine of corruption. The basest expediency had been the governing principle of statesmen and lawyers; the most abject servility had been the leading creed of divines. Loyalty always wore the livery of the menial. Patriotism was ever flaunting the badges of faction. The bulk of the people were unmoved by any proud resentments or eager hopes. They went on in their course of industrious occupation, without much caring whether they were under an absolute or a constitutional government, as long as they could eat, drink, and be merry. They*

had got rid of the Puritan severity; and if decency was outraged in the Court and laughed at on the stage, there was greater license for popular indulgences.

The leading statesmen were too often utterly untruthful, and ready to take bribes. The judges were, as a rule, mean, corrupt, ignorant creatures of the Court. The Church of England, which ought to have been a bulwark against wickedness, had never recovered the suicidal loss of its life-blood caused by the Act of Uniformity in 1662, and was a weak, timid, servile body. The bishops and clergy, with a few brilliant exceptions, were very unlike the Reformers, and always unwilling to find fault with any great man, or to dispute the Divine right of kings to do as they pleased.

The Dissenters were crushed to the earth by petty intolerant restrictions; and, between fines, imprisonments and persecutions, were little able to do anything to mend the times, and could barely keep their heads above water.

Last, but not least, we must not forget that for at least a hundred years England had been incessantly exposed to the untiring machinations of the Jesuits. Ever since the accession of Elizabeth, those mischievous agents of Popery had been compassing sea and land to undo the work of the Reformation, and to bring back our country to the thraldom of the Church of Rome. Disguised in every possible way, and professing anything by the Pope's permission and dispensation, in order to accomplish their end, these Jesuits throughout the days of the Stuarts were incessantly at work. To set Churchmen against Dissenters, Calvinists against Arminians, sect against sect, party against party, and so to weaken the Protestant cause, was their one constant employment. How much of the bitter divisions between Churchmen and Nonconformists, how much of the religious strife which defiled the early part of the seventeenth century is owing to the Jesuits, I believe the last day alone will declare. Those only who read Panzani's *Memoirs*, or Dean Goode's *Rome's Tactics*, can have any idea of the mischief they did.

In short, if there ever was an era in modern history when a Popish

King of England could promote Popery and do deeds of astounding cruelty and injustice without let or hindrance, that era was the reign of James II. What might have been the final result, with such a king and such a field of action, if he had not gone too fast and overshot his mark, is impossible to say. God in his infinite goodness had mercy on England, and delivered us from his wicked designs. But the things that he did, while he reigned,[69] and the singular manner in which he at last over-reached himself by the trial of the Seven Bishops, and lost his throne, ought never to be forgotten by any Englishman who is a true Protestant and loves his country.

James' attempt to pull down Protestantism

There are five leading events, or salient points, in this reign, which are specially worth remembering. They follow each other in regular order, from the accession of James to his abdication. One common aim and object underlaid them all—that aim was to pull down Protestantism and to plant Popery on its ruins.

James' treatment of nonconformists

The first disgraceful page in the history of James II's reign is his savage and brutal treatment of the Nonconformists and Dissenters. Our great historian, Macaulay, says: "He hated the Puritan sect with a manifold hatred, theological and political, hereditary and personal. He regarded them as the foes of heaven as well as the foes of all legitimate authority in Church and State."[70] The plain truth is, that James, with all his natural dullness of character, had sense enough to know that for many years the most decided and zealous advocates of Protestantism had been the Nonconformists, and that when Churchmen under Archbishop Laud's mischievous influence had become lukewarm, Nonconformists had been the most inveterate enemies of Popery. Knowing this, he began his reign

---

69 Those who wish to make themselves acquainted with the reign of James II would do well to study Burnet, Hallam, Macaulay, Charles Knight, Ranke, and Stoughton's *History of the Church of the Restoration*.

70 Macaulay, volume 1, page 494.

by attempting to crush the Nonconformists entirely. If his predecessors had chastised them with rods, he tried to chastise them with scorpions (1 Kings 12:11). If he could not convert them, he would silence them by prosecutions, fines, and imprisonments, and, like Pharaoh, "make their lives grievous" by hard measures. He argued, no doubt, that, if he could only stop the mouths of the Nonconformists, he would soon make short work of the Church of England, and he cunningly began with the weaker party. In both cases, happily, he reckoned without his host.

To describe how the unhappy Nonconformists at that period were summoned, fined, silenced, driven from their homes, and allowed no rest for the sole of their foot, would be an endless task. Two pictures will suffice to give an idea of the treatment to which they were subjected. One picture shall be taken from England, and the other from Scotland. Each picture shows things which happened with the King's sanction within three months after he came to the throne.

The English picture is the so-called trial of Baxter, the famous author of *The Saint's Rest*, a book which is deservedly held in honour down to this day. Baxter was tried at Westminster Hall before James' detestable tool, Chief Justice Jeffreys, in May 1685. He was charged with having published seditious matter reflecting on the bishops, in his *Paraphrase on the New Testament*. A more absurd and unfounded accusation could not have been made. The book is still extant, and any one will see at a glance that there was no ground for the charge. From the very opening of the trial it was clear which way the verdict was intended to go. The Lord Chief Justice of England behaved as if he were counsel for the prosecution and not judge. He used abusive language towards the defendant, such as was more suited to Billingsgate than a court of law; while the counsel for the defence were brow-beaten, silenced, and put down, or else interrupted by violent invectives against their client. At one stage the Lord Chief Justice exclaimed: "This is an old rogue who hath poisoned the world with his Kidderminster doctrines. He encouraged all the women and maids to bring their bodkins and thimbles to carry on war against the King of ever blessed memory. An old schismatical knave! A hypocritical villain!"

By and by he called Baxter "an old blockhead, an unthankful villain, a conceited, stubborn, fanatical dog." "Hang him!" he said, "this one old fellow hath cast more reproaches on the constitution and discipline of our Church than will be wiped off for a hundred years. But I'll handle him for it; for he deserves to be whipped through the city." Shortly afterwards, when Baxter began to say a few words on his own behalf, Jeffreys stopped him, crying out: "Richard, Richard, dost thou think we'll hear thee poison the court? Richard, thou art an old fellow, and an old knave; thou hast written books enough to load a cart, every one as full of sedition, I might say of treason, as an egg is full of meat. Hadst thou been whipped out of thy writing trade forty years ago, it had been happy." It is needless to say in such a court as this Baxter was at once found guilty. He was fined five hundred marks, which it was known he could not pay; condemned to lie in prison till he paid it, and bound over to good behaviour for seven years. And the issue of the matter was that the holy author of *The Saint's Rest*, a poor, old, diseased, childless widower, lay for two years in Southwark gaol.

The Scotch picture of the Nonconformists' sufferings under James II is even blacker than the English one. I shall take it substantially from Wodrow's and Macaulay's history. In the very same month that Baxter was tried, two women named Margaret Maclachlan and Margaret Wilson, the former an aged widow, the latter a girl of eighteen, suffered death for their religion in Wigtonshire, at the hands of James II's myrmidons. They were both godly women, innocent of any crime but Nonconformity. They were offered their lives if they would abjure the cause of the insurgent covenanters, and attend the Episcopal worship. They both refused; and they were sentenced to be drowned. They were carried to a spot on the shore of the Solway Firth, which the tide overflowed twice a day, and were fastened to stakes fixed in the sand between high and low water-mark. The elder woman was placed nearest to the advancing water, in the hopes that her last agonies might terrify the younger one into submission. The sight was dreadful.

But the courage of the young survivor did not fail. She saw her fellow-sufferer drowned, and saw the sea draw nearer and nearer to herself, but gave no signs of alarm. She prayed and sang verses of Psalms, till the waves choked her voice. When she had tasted the bitterness of death, she was, by cruel mercy, unbound and restored to life. When she came to herself, pitying friends and neighbours implored her to yield. "Dear Margaret," they cried, "only say, 'God save the King.'" The poor girl, true to her theology, gasped out, "May God save him if it be God's will." Her friends crowded round the presiding officer, crying, "She has said it, indeed, sir, she has said it." "Will she take the abjuration?" he sternly demanded. "Never," she exclaimed. "I am Christ's; let me go." And once more bound to the stake, the waters of the Solway closed over her for the last time. Her epitaph may be seen to this day in Wigton churchyard.

Such were the dealings of James with Protestant Nonconformists at the beginning of his reign. I make no comment on them. These two examples speak for themselves; and they do not stand alone. The story of the murder of John Brown of Priesthill, by Claverhouse, is as sad as that of Margaret Wilson. No wonder that a deep dislike to Episcopacy is rooted down in the hearts of Scotch people to this very day! They never forget such stories as Margaret Wilson's. Even in England I wish I could add that vile prosecutions like that of Baxter had called forth any expression of disapproval from English Churchmen. But, alas! for a season, James persecuted and prospered, and no man opposed him.

James' cruelty towards Monmouth's rebellion

The second black page in the history of James II's reign is the detestable cruelty with which he punished those English counties which had taken any part in Monmouth's rebellion, in the autumn of 1685. Concerning that miserable rebellion there can, of course, be but one opinion among sensible men. It is vain to deny that the brief insurrection, which ended with the battle of Sedgemoor, was an enormous folly as well as a crime. We all know how Monmouth, its unhappy leader, paid for it by dying on the scaffold. But it is equally vain to deny that the bloodthirsty ferocity with which James avenged himself on all who had favoured Monmouth's cause, or taken arms in his support, is unparalleled in the annals of English history.

The proceedings of that military monster, Colonel Kirke, immediately after the defeat and dispersion of the rebel army, surpassed anything that we heard of in the Indian Mutiny. At Taunton he is said to have hanged at least a hundred so-called rebels within a week after the battle of Sedgemoor, and many without even the form of a trial. Not a few of his wretched victims were quartered, and their heads and limbs sent to be hanged in chains in the neighbouring villages. "So many dead bodies were quartered," says Macaulay, "that the executioner under the gallows stood ankle deep in blood."[71]

But even the diabolical cruelties of Colonel Kirke were surpassed by the execrable sentences of Judge Jeffreys, when he went on Circuit to the Assizes in Hampshire, Dorset, and Somerset, two months after the battle of Sedgemoor. In Dorset he hanged about seventy, in Somerset no less than two hundred and thirty-three. The number of those transported for life was 841. The greater part of these were poor ignorant rustics, many of them men of blameless private character, who had taken arms under the idea that Protestantism was at stake; and they died for no other offence than that of simply following Monmouth, a political adventurer, for a few short weeks. The Assize was long known as the bloody Assize. "In Somersetshire," says Macaulay, "on the green of every large village which had furnished Monmouth with soldiers, ironed corpses clattering in the wind, or human heads and quarters stuck on poles poisoned the air, and made the traveller sick with horror. In many parishes the peasantry could not even assemble in God's house without seeing the ghastly face of some neighbour's skull grinning at them on the porch." In Hampshire, Jeffreys actually sentenced to death a venerable old lady named Lady Lisle, aged above seventy, for no other crime than that of affording temporary shelter to an insurgent; and nothing but the indignant remonstrance of the Winchester clergy prevented her being burned alive. Lord Feversham, the conqueror of Sedgemoor, and

---

71 Macaulay, volume 1, page 629.

Lord Clarendon, the King's brother-in-law, in vain interceded for her. Jeffreys was allowed to work his will, and she was actually beheaded in Winchester market-place.

For all this abominable cruelty, James II must always be held responsible. The vile agents who shed this blood were his tools, and he had only to speak the word and the work of death would have ceased. Hallam, the historian, expressly says that the King was the author of all this bloodshed, and that Jeffreys afterward declared "he had not been bloody enough for his employer."[72] But the real secret of the King's savage and detestable conduct was a determination to put down Protestantism by a reign of terror, and deter men from any future movement in its favour. And, after all, the truth must be spoken. James was a bigoted member of a Church which for ages has been too often "drunken with the blood of saints and the martyrs of Jesus." He only walked in the steps of the Duke of Alva in the Netherlands; in the steps of Charles IX at the massacre of St. Bartholomew; in the steps of the Duke of Savoy in Piedmont, until Cromwell interfered and obliged him to cease; and in the steps of the hateful Spanish Inquisition. One thing is very certain: there never was a petty insurrection so ruthlessly quenched in blood as Monmouth's rebellion was quenched by James the Papist. Blood makes a great stain. He found to his cost one day that the blood shed by Kirke and Jeffreys with his sanction had cried to heaven, and was not forgotten. When the Prince of Orange landed at Torbay, the western counties joined him to a man, and forsook James.

James' attempt to silence preachers

The third black page in the history of James II's reign was his daring attempt to gag the pulpit, and stop the mouths of all who preached against Popery.

Preaching in every age of the Church has always been God's chief instrument for setting forward religious truth, and checking error. Preaching was one principal agency by which the great work of the Reformation

---

72 Hallam, volume 3, page 93.

was effected in England. The Church of Rome knows that full well and, wherever she dares, she has always endeavoured to exalt ceremonials and to depreciate the pulpit. To use old Latimer's quaint words, "Whenever the devil gets into a church, his plan is to cry, 'Up with candles and down with preaching.'" Next to an open and free Bible, the greatest obstacle to the progress of Popery is a free pulpit, and the public exposition of God's Word. That James II, like all thorough-going Papists, knew all this, we cannot doubt for a moment. We need not, therefore, wonder that in 1686 he commenced an attack on the English pulpit. If he could once silence that mighty organ, he hoped to pave the way for the advance of Popery. "He took on himself," says Macaulay—

> To charge the clergy of the Established Church to abstain from touching on controverted points of doctrine in their discourses. Thus, while sermons in defence of the Roman Catholic religion were preached every Sunday and holiday in the Royal Chapel, the Church of the State, the Church of the great majority of the nation, was forbidden to explain and vindicate her own principles.[73]

William Sherlock, Master of the Temple, was the first to feel the royal displeasure. His pension was stopped, and he was severely reprimanded. John Sharpe, Dean of Norwich, and Rector of St. Giles', gave even greater offence. In reply to an appeal from a parishioner, he delivered an animated discourse against the pretensions of the Church of Rome. Compton, the Bishop of London, was immediately ordered to suspend him, and on his objecting to do so, he was himself suspended from all spiritual functions, and the charge of his diocese was committed to two time-serving prelates named Spratt and Crewe. Compton was already famous for his dislike to Popery: when James came to the throne he had boldly declared in the House of Lords that "the Constitution was in danger." We can well understand that James was anxious to suppress him.[74]

Singularly enough, this high-handed proceeding worked round for

---

73 Macaulay, volume 2, page 91.

74 See Ranke, volume 4, page 277.

good. For the first time since his accession to the throne, James received a distinct check. The attacks on Sherlock, Sharpe, and Bishop Compton, roused the spirit of the whole body of the English clergy. To preach against the errors of Popery was now regarded as a point of honour and duty. The London clergy set an example which was bravely followed all over the country. The King's prohibition to handle controversial subjects was everywhere disregarded. It was impossible to punish an offence which was committed every Sunday by thousands of divines from the Isle of Wight to Berwick-upon-Tweed, and from the Land's End to the North Foreland. Moreover, the spirit of the congregations was thoroughly roused. There were old men living in London whose grandfathers had heard Latimer preach, and had seen John Rogers burnt at Smithfield. There were others whose parents had seen Laud beheaded for trying to Romanize the Church and prosecuting Protestant Churchmen. Such men as these were thoroughly stirred and disgusted by James's movement; and if the clergy had been silent about Popery, they would have resented their silence as unfaithfulness and sin.

The printing-presses, besides, both at London, Oxford, and Cambridge, poured forth a constant stream of anti-Popish literature, and supplied all who could read with ample information about every error of the Church of Rome. Tillotson, Stillingfleet, Sherlock, Patrick, Tenison, Wake, Fowler, Clagett and many others wrote numerous treatises of all kinds to expose Popery, which exist to this day, and which at the time produced an immense effect. Many of these are to be found in the three huge folios called *Gibson's Preservative*, and Macaulay estimates that as many as 20,000 pages of them are to be found in the British Museum.

The whole affair is a striking instance of God's power to bring good out of evil. The very step by which this unhappy Popish monarch thought to silence his strongest foe proved the first step towards his own ruin. Up to this date he seemed to carry everything before him. From this date he began to fall. From the moment he put forth his hand to touch the ark, to interfere with the word of God, to silence its preachers, he never prospered, and every succeeding step in his reign was in the downward direction. Like Haman, he had dared to meddle with God's peculiar servants, and like Haman he fell, never to rise again (see Esther 9:24-25).

James' interference at Oxford and Cambridge Universities

The fourth black page in the history of James II's reign is his tyrannical invasion of the rights of the two great Universities of Oxford and Cambridge in 1687.

The influence of these two venerable bodies in England has always been very great, and I trust they will always be so governed that it will never become less. But it is no exaggeration to say that it never was so great as towards the end of the seventeenth century. Beside them there were no universities or colleges. King's College, London; University College, Durham; St. Aidan's; Highbury; St. Bees, and Cuddesdon did not exist. Oxford and Cambridge stood alone. They were the fountains of all the learning of the day, and the training school of all the ablest divines and lawyers, poets, and orators of the land. Even among the Puritans it would be hard to find any man of ability who had not begun his career and picked up his first knowledge at some college in Oxford or Cambridge. In short, the two Universities were the intellectual heart of England, and every pulsation of that heart was felt throughout the kingdom.

All this, we need not doubt, even the dull mind of James II clearly perceived. He saw that he had little chance of Romanizing England until he could get hold of the two Universities, and this he resolved to try. He was encouraged, probably, to make the attempt by the notorious loyalty to the House of Stuart which Oxford and Cambridge had always exhibited. Both the Universities had suffered heavily for their attachment to the King's side during the unhappy Commonwealth wars. Many a Head of a College had been displaced and his position filled by one of Cromwell's Puritans. Owen had ruled at Christ Church and Goodwin at Magdalen. Many a College plate-chest was sadly empty compared to its state in olden times, having given up its silver to be melted down in aid of Charles I, and to buy arms and ammunition. Ever since the Reformation, the two Universities had exhibited the most obsequious subserviency to the

Crown, had stoutly maintained the divine right of kings, and had often approached the throne in addresses full of fulsome adulation. I believe that James flattered himself that they would go on yielding everything to his will, and fondly dreamed that in a few years they would be completely under the Pope's command, and the education of young England would be in the hands of the Church of Rome. It was a grand and intoxicating prospect. But he reckoned without his host. He little knew the spirit that was yet left by the Isis and the Cam.

James opened his campaign and crossed the Rubicon by attacking the University of Cambridge. The law was clear and distinct, that no person should be admitted to any degree without taking the "Oath of Supremacy," and another oath called the "Oath of Obedience." Nevertheless, in February 1687, a royal letter was sent to Cambridge directing that a Benedictine monk, named Alban Francis, should be admitted as Master of Arts. Between reverence for the King and reverence for their own statutes, the academical officers were naturally placed in a most perplexing position. To their infinite credit they took the right course, and steadily refused to admit the King's nominee unless he took the oaths.

The result was that the Vice-Chancellor of Cambridge was summoned to appear before the New Court of High Commission, presided over by Jeffreys, together with deputies appointed by the Senate. When the day arrived, Dr. Pechell, the Vice-Chancellor, a man of no particular vigour or ability, accompanied by eight distinguished men, of whom the famous Isaac Newton was one, appeared before this formidable tribunal. Their case was as clear as daylight. They offered to prove that they had done nothing contrary to law and practice, and had only carried out the plain meaning of their statutes. But Jeffreys would hear nothing. He treated the whole party with as much vulgar insolence as if they were felons being tried before him at the Old Bailey, and they were thrust out of court without a hearing. They were soon called in and informed that the Commission had determined to deprive Pechell of the Vice-Chancellorship, and to suspend him from all the emoluments to which he was entitled as Master of a College. "As for you," said Jeffreys to Isaac Newton and his seven companions, with disgusting levity, "I send you home with a text of Scripture, 'Go your way and sin no more, lest a worse thing come upon you.'"

From Cambridge James turned to Oxford. Here, it must be avowed, he began his operations with great advantages. Popery had already effected a lodgment in the citadel, and got allies in the heart of the University. Already a Roman Catholic named Massey had been made Dean of Christ Church by the nomination of the Crown, and the House had submitted. Already University College was little better than a Romish seminary by the perversion of the Master, Obadiah Walker, to Popery. Mass was daily said in both Colleges. But this state of things had caused an immense amount of smouldering dissatisfaction throughout Oxford. The undergraduates hooted Walker's congregation, and chanted satirical ballads under his windows without the interference of Proctors. The burden of one of their songs has been preserved to this day, and you might have heard at night in High Street, near the fine old college, such words as these:—

Here old Obadiah
Sings Ave Maria.

In short, any careful observer might have foreseen that Oxford feeling towards the King was undergoing a great change, and that it would take very little to create a blaze.

Just at this crisis, the President of Magdalen College died and it became the duty of the Fellows, according to their statutes, to elect a successor, either from their own society or from New College. With an astounding mixture of folly and audacity, the King actually recommended the Fellows to elect to the vacant place a man named Anthony Farmer, a person of infamous moral character, utterly destitute of any claim to govern a college; a drunkard, a Papist, and a person disqualified by the statutes of Waynflete, as he was neither Fellow of New College nor of Magdalen. To their infinite credit the Fellows of Magdalen, by an overwhelming majority, refused to elect the King's nominee, resolved to face his displeasure, and deliberately chose for their President a man named John Hough, a Fellow of eminent virtue and prudence.

At once they were treated with the utmost violence, injustice, and indignity. The King insisted on their accepting another President of his own selection, and commanded them to take a mean creature of the Court named Parker, Bishop of Oxford. The Fellows firmly refused, saying they had lawfully elected Hough, and they would have no other President. In vain they were threatened and insulted, first by the King himself, and then by a Special Commission sent down from London. They stood firm, and would not give way one inch. The Commission finally pronounced Hough an intruder, dismissed him from his presidency, and charged the Fellows no longer to recognise his authority, but to assist at the admission of the Bishop of Oxford.

It was then that the gallant Hough publicly addressed the following remarkable words to the Commission: "My Lords, you have this day deprived me of my freehold. I hereby protest against all your proceedings as illegal, unjust, and null, and I appeal from you to our sovereign Lord the King in his Courts of Justice." But though thus driven from his office by force, Hough was backed by the general feeling of the whole University, and of almost everyone connected with Magdalen. At the installation of his successor (Parker) only two Fellows out of forty attended the ceremony. The college porter, Robert Gardner, threw down his keys. The butler refused to scratch Hough's name out of the buttery books. No blacksmith in all the city of Oxford could be found to force the locks of the President's lodge, and the Commissioners were obliged to employ their own servants to break open the doors with iron bars.

But the matter did not end here. On the day that Hough was expelled from his Presidency and Parker installed, the Commissioners invited the Vice-Chancellor of 1687 to dine with them. The Vice-Chancellor that year was Gilbert Ironside, Warden of Wadham, and afterwards Bishop of Hereford. He refused. "My taste," he said, "differs from that of Colonel Kirke's. I cannot eat my meals with appetite under a gallows." The

Scholars of Magdalen refused to pull off their caps to the new ruler of Magdalen. The Demies[75] refused to perform their academical exercises and attend lectures, saying that they were deprived of their lawful governor, and would submit to no usurped authority. Attempts were made to bribe them by the offer of some of the lucrative fellowships declared vacant. But one undergraduate after another refused, and one who did accept was turned out of the Hall by the rest. The expulsion of the Fellows was followed by the expulsion of a crowd of Demies. A few weeks after this Parker died, some said of mortification and a broken heart. He was buried in the antechapel of Magdalen; but no stone marks his grave. Then the King's whole plan was carried into effect. The College was turned into a Popish seminary, and Bonaventura Giffard, a Roman Catholic Bishop, was made President. In one day, twelve Papists were made Fellows. The Roman Catholic service was performed in the chapel, and the whole work of violence and spoliation was completed.

Such were the dealings of James II with Oxford and Cambridge. Their gross injustice was only equalled by their gross impolicy. In his furious zeal for Popery, the King completely over-reached himself. He alienated the affections of the two most powerful educational institutions in the land, and filled the hearts of thousands of the ablest minds in England with a deep sense of wrong. And when the end came, as it did within eighteen months, he found that no places deserted his cause so readily as the two over which he had ridden roughshod, the two great English Universities of Oxford and Cambridge.

James' alienation of the nobility and gentry

The fifth dark page in the history of James II's reign is his rash attempt to trample down the English nobility and gentry in the counties, and substitute for them servile creatures of his own who would help forward his designs.

In order to understand this move of the misguided King, it must be remembered that he wanted to get a new House of Commons, a House

---

75 Demies are foundation scholars of Magdalen College—*Editor.*

which would do his bidding and not oppose his Romanizing plans. He knew enough of England to be aware that ever since the days of Simon de Montfort every intelligent Englishman has attached great importance to an elected Parliament. He had not entirely forgotten the iron hand of the Long Parliament in his father's days. He rightly judged that he would never succeed in overthrowing Protestantism without the sanction of a House of Commons, and that sanction he resolved to try to obtain.

"Having determined to pack a Parliament," says Macaulay, "James set himself energetically and methodically to the work. A proclamation appeared in the *Gazette*" (at the end of 1687) "announcing that the King had determined to revise the Commissions of Peace and of Lieutenancy, and to retain in public employment only such gentlemen as would support his policy." At the same time a Committee of Seven Privy Councillors sat at Whitehall, including Father Petre, an ambitious Jesuit, for the purpose of "regulating," as it was called, all the municipal corporations in boroughs:—

> *The persons on whom James principally relied for assistance [continues Macaulay], were the Lord Lieutenants. Every Lord Lieutenant received written orders directing him to go down immediately into his county. There he was to summon before him all his deputies, and all the Justices of the Peace, and to put to them a set of interrogatories framed for the purpose of finding out how they would act at a general election. He was to take down their answers in writing, and transmit them to the Government. He was to furnish a list of such Romanists and Protestant Dissenters as were best qualified for commissions as magistrates, and for command in the militia. He was also to examine the state of all the boroughs in his county, and to make such reports as might be needful to guide the London board of regulators. And it was intimated to each Lord Lieutenant that he must perform these duties himself, and not delegate them to any other person.*

The first effect of these audacious and unconstitutional orders might have opened the eyes of any king of common sense. The spirit of the old

Barons who met at Runnymede proved to be not extinct. Even before this time the Duke of Norfolk had stopped at the door of the Popish chapel which James attended, and when James remonstrated and said, "Your Grace's father would have gone farther," had boldly replied, "Your Majesty's father would not have gone so far." But now it became clear that many other peers beside the Duke of Norfolk were Protestant to the backbone. Half the Lord Lieutenants in England flatly refused to do the King's dirty work, and to stoop to the odious service imposed on them. They were immediately dismissed, and inferior men, of more pliant and supple consciences, were pitchforked into their places.

The list of high-minded noblemen who resisted the King's will on this memorable occasion is even now most remarkable, and deserves to be had in remembrance. One great name follows another in grand succession in Macaulay's pages, until one's breath is almost taken away by the sight of the King's folly. In Essex, the Earl of Oxford; in Staffordshire, the Earl of Shrewsbury; in Sussex, the Earl of Dorset; in Yorkshire, the Duke of Somerset in the East Riding, and Lord Fauconberg in the North Riding; in Shropshire, Lord Newport; in Lancashire, the Earl of Derby; in Wiltshire, the Earl of Pembroke; in Leicestershire, the Earl of Rutland; in Buckinghamshire, the Earl of Bridgwater; in Cumberland, the Earl of Thanet; in Warwickshire, the Earl of Northampton; in Oxfordshire, the Earl of Abingdon; in Derbyshire, the Earl of Scarsdale; and in Hampshire, the Earl of Gainsborough—all were summarily sent to the rightabout; and for what? Simply, as every one knew, because they preferred a good conscience to Crown favour, principle to place, and Protestantism to Popery. The gallant words of the Earl of Oxford, who was turned out in Essex, when the King demanded an explanation of his refusal to obey, spoke the sentiments of all: "Sir, I will stand by your Majesty against all enemies to the last drop of blood; but this is a matter of conscience, and I cannot comply."

A viler piece of ingratitude than this move of James can hardly be conceived. Most of the noblemen whom he dismissed were the representatives of great families who, in the Commonwealth wars, made immense sacrifices in his father's cause. Some of them, like the Earl of Derby, could tell of fathers and grandfathers who had died for King Charles. Many of them could show swords and helmets hanging over their Elizabethan fireplaces which had been notched and dented in fighting against the Parliamentary forces at Edgehill, Marston Moor, and Naseby. Not a few of them could point to ruined castles and halls, to parks despoiled of their timber, plate-chests emptied of their contents, and properties sadly impoverished in the days when Cavaliers fought against Roundheads. And now, forsooth, the son of the martyred Charles, as they had fondly called him, turned round upon them, trampled on their feelings, and required them to lie down, and let him walk over their consciences. Can we wonder that they keenly resented the King's conduct! At one fell swoop he destroyed the affection of half the leading men in the English counties, and from being his friends they became his foes.

In fact, the ingratitude of the King was now only equalled by his folly and impolicy. No sooner was his new machinery for packing a subservient Parliament put in motion, than it broke down and utterly failed. From every corner of the realm there came the tidings of failure. The new Lord Lieutenants could do nothing. The Magistrates and candidates for Parliament evaded inquiries, and refused to pledge themselves to do the King's will. Arguments, promises, and threats were alike in vain. A deep-rooted suspicion had got into men's minds that James wanted to subvert Protestantism, and re-introduce Popery, and they would not give way. From Norfolk, the Duke of Norfolk reported that out of seventy leading gentlemen in the county only six held out any hopes of supporting the Court. In Hertfordshire the Squires told Lord Rochester that they would send no man to Parliament who would vote for taking away the safeguards of the Protestant religion. The gentry of Bucks, Shropshire, and Wiltshire held the same language.

The Magistrates and Deputy-Lieutenants of Cornwall and Devonshire told Lord Bath, without a dissenting voice, that they would sacrifice life and property for the Crown, but that the Protestant religion was dearer to them than either. "And, Sir," said Lord Bath to the King, "if your

Majesty dismisses them, their successors would give the same answer." In Lancashire, a very Romish county, the new Lord Lieutenant reported that one-third of the Magistrates were opposed to the Court. In Hampshire the whole of the Magistrates, excepting five or six, declared they would take no part in the civil or military government of the county while the King was represented there by the Duke of Berwick, a Papist.

The sum of the whole matter is this. The attack of James on the independence of the county gentry and nobility was as completely a failure as his attack on the pulpit and the Universities. It was worse than this. It sowed the seeds of disaffection to his person from one end of England to the other, and alienated from him thousands of leading men who, under other circumstances, would perhaps have stood by him to the last. And the result was, that when the Prince of Orange landed at Torbay a year afterwards, he found friends in half the counties in England. By the overruling providence of God and his own judicial blindness, James paved the way to his own ruin. "The Thanes fell from him." The nobility, one after another, forsook him, and he was left friendless and alone.

The Prosecution of the Seven Bishops

I come now to the closing scene in King James' disgraceful reign, the prosecution and trial of the Seven Bishops. The importance of that event is so great, and the consequences which resulted from it were so immense, that I must enter somewhat fully into its details. I do so the more willingly because attempts are sometimes made nowadays to misrepresent this trial, to place the motives of the bishops in a wrong light, and to obscure the real issues which were at stake. Some men will do anything in these times to mystify the public mind, to pervert history, and to whitewash the Church of Rome. But I have made it my business to search up every authority I can find about this era. I have no doubt whatever what is the true account of the whole affair. And I shall try to set before my readers the "thing as it is."

The origin of the trial of the Seven Bishops was a proclamation put forth by James II, on the 27th of April 1688, called the "Declaration of Indulgence." It was a Declaration which differed little from one put forth in April 1687. But it was followed by an "Order of Council" that it was to be read on two successive Sundays, in Divine Service, by all the officiating ministers in all the churches and chapels of the kingdom. In London the reading was to take place on the 20th and 27th of May, and in other parts of England on the 3rd and 10th of June. The bishops were directed to distribute copies of the Declaration throughout their respective dioceses. The substance of the Declaration was short and simple. It suspended all penal laws against Nonconformists. It authorized both Roman Catholics and Protestant Dissenters to perform their worship publicly. It forbade the King's subjects, on pain of his displeasure, to molest any assembly. It abrogated all those Acts of Parliament which imposed any religious test as a qualification for any civil or military office.

To us, the Declaration may seem very reasonable and harmless. To the England of the seventeenth century it wore a very different aspect! Men knew the hand from which it came, and saw the latent intention. Under the specious plea of toleration and liberty, the object of the Declaration was to advance Popery and give license and free scope to the Church of Rome, and to all its schemes for reconquering England.

This famous Declaration, we can see at a glance, placed the bishops and clergy in a most awkward position. What were they to do? What was the path of duty? They were thoroughly pinned on the horns of a dilemma. If they refused compliance to the King's wishes they would seem intolerant, illiberal, and unkind to the Nonconformists, as well as disloyal, disrespectful, and disobedient to their sovereign. If they yielded to the King's wishes, and read the Declaration, they would be assisting the propagation of Popery. The liberty James wanted them to proclaim was neither more nor less than indulgence to the Jesuits and the whole Church of Rome. In short, they found themselves between Scylla and Charybdis, and could not possibly avoid giving offence. Refusing to sanction the Declaration, they would certainly displease the King and perhaps irritate the Dissenters. Consenting to it, they would infallibly help the Pope. Never, perhaps, were English bishops and clergy placed in such a difficult and perplexing position!

God's ways, however, are not as man's ways, and light often arises out of darkness in quarters where it was not expected. At this critical juncture the Nonconformists, to their eternal honour, came forward and cut the knot, and helped the bishops to a right decision. The shrewd sons of the good old Puritans saw clearly what James meant. They saw that under a specious pretence of liberty, he wanted a fulcrum for a lever which would turn England upside down, and destroy the work of the Reformation. Like the noble-minded Roman ambassador before Pyrrhus, who was shown first a bag of gold, and then an elephant, they refused to be bribed just as they had formerly refused to be intimidated. They would have none of the Royal indulgence, if it could only be purchased at the expense of the nation's Protestantism. Baxter, and Bates, and Howe, and the great bulk of the London Nonconformists, entreated the clergy to stand firm, and not to yield one inch to the King. Young Defoe said to his Nonconformist brethren, "I had rather the Church of England should pull our clothes off by fines and forfeitures, than the Papists should fall both upon the Church and the Dissenters, and pull our skins off by fire and faggot."[76]

Oliver Heywood, a famous Nonconformist of the day, says distinctly in his account of the times, "though the Dissenters had liberty promised, we knew it was not out of love to us, but for another purpose. We heard the King had said he was forced to grant liberty at present to those whom his soul abhorred."[77]

The immediate result was that a meeting of the London clergy was held, and after much debate, in which Tillotson, Sherlock, Patrick, and Stillingfleet took part, it was decided that the "Order in Council" should not be obeyed. No one contributed to this result more than Dr. Fowler, Vicar of St. Giles, Cripplegate, a well-known Broad Churchman. While

---

76 C. Knight, *History*, volume 4, page 419.

77 Heywood's *Works*, volume 1, page 287.

the matter yet hung in the balance, and the final vote seemed doubtful, he rose and said: "I must be plain. The question to my mind is so simple, that argument can throw no new light on it, and can only beget heat. Let every man say Yes or No. But I cannot consent to be bound by the majority. I shall be sorry to cause a breach of unity. But this Declaration I cannot read." This bold speech turned the scale. A resolution by which all present pledged themselves not to read the Declaration was drawn up, and was ultimately signed by eighty-five incumbents in London.

In the meantime the Archbishop of Canterbury, William Sancroft, showed himself not unequal to the emergency. He was naturally a cautious, quiet, and somewhat timid man, and the last person to be combative, and to quarrel with kings. Nevertheless he came out nobly and well, and rose to the occasion. As soon as the Order in Council appeared, he summoned to Lambeth Palace those few bishops, divines, and laymen who happened to be in London and took counsel with them. It was resolved to resist the King, and to refuse to read the Declaration. The Primate then wrote to all the bishops on the English bench on whom he could depend, and urged them to come up to London at once, and join him in a formal protest and petition. But time was short. There were no railways in those days. Journeying was slow work. Eighteen bishops, says Burnet, agreed with Sancroft.[78] But with the utmost exertion only six bishops could get to London in time to help the Primate. These six, with the Archbishop at their head, assembled at Lambeth on the 18th of May, only two days before the fatal Sunday, when the King's Declaration was to be read in London, and before night agreed on a petition or protest to which all affixed their names.

The names of the six bishops who signed this remarkable document, beside Sancroft, deserve to be known and remembered. They were as follows: Lloyd of St. Asaph, Turner of Ely, Lake of Chichester, Ken of Bath and Wells, White of Peterborough, and Sir Jonathan Trelawney of Bristol. It is a curious fact that, with the single exception of Ken, the author of *Morning and Evening Hymns*, not one of the seven men who

---

78 Burnet, *The History of My Own Time*, volume 3, page 266.

signed the petition could be called a remarkable man in any way. Not one, beside Ken, has made any mark in the theological world, or lives as a writer or preacher. Not one of the whole seven could be named in the same breath with Parker, or Whitgift, or Grindal, or Jewel, or Andrews, or Hall. They were probably respectable, worthy, quiet, old-fashioned High Churchmen; and that was all. But God loves to be glorified by using weak instruments. Whatever they were in other respects, they were of one mind in seeing the danger which threatened Protestantism, and in determination to stand by it to the death. It was not jealousy of Dissenters but dislike to Popery, be it remembered, which actuated their conduct and knit them together.[79] All honour be to them. They have supplied an unanswerable proof that the real, loyal, honest, old-fashioned High Churchmen disliked Popery as much as any school in the Church.

The famous petition which the Seven Bishops drew up and signed on this occasion is a curious document. It is short, and tame, and cautious, and somewhat clumsily composed. But the worthy composers, no doubt, were pressed for time, and had no leisure to polish their sentences. Moreover, we know that they acted under the best advice, and were careful not to say too much and give needless offence.

> *In substance (says Macaulay) nothing could be more skilfully framed. All disloyalty, all intolerance, were reverently disclaimed. The King was assured that the Church was still, as ever, faithful to the throne. He was also assured that the bishops, in proper time and place, would, as Lords of Parliament and members of the Upper House of Convocation, show they were by no means wanting in tenderness for the conscientious scruples of Dissenters. The Parliament, both in the late and present reign, had pronounced that the Sovereign was not constitutionally competent to dispense with statutes in matters ecclesiastical. The Declaration was therefore illegal, and the Petitioners could not in prudence, honour, or conscience, be parties to the solemn publication of an illegal Declaration in the House of God, and during the time of Divine Service.*

---

79 Ranke, volume 4, page 346.

Pointless and tame as the Petition may seem to us, we must not allow ourselves to make any mistake as to the latent meaning of the document and the real object of the bishops in refusing to obey the King. We must do them justice. They were thoroughly convinced that the Declaration was intended to help Popery, and they were determined to make a stand and resist it. They had no ill-feeling towards Dissenters, and no desire to continue their disabilities. But they saw clearly that the whole cause of Protestantism was in jeopardy, and that, now or never, they must risk everything to defend it. Every historian of any worth acknowledges this, and it is vain to try to take any other view, unless we are prepared to write history anew. A cloud of witnesses agree here. There is an overwhelming mass of evidence to prove that the real reason why the Seven Bishops resolved to oppose the King, was their determination to maintain the principles of the Reformation and to oppose any further movement towards Rome. In one word, the cause for which they boldly nailed their colours to the mast was the good old cause of Protestantism versus Popery. Every one, Churchman or Dissenter, knew that in 1688, and it is a grievous shame that any one now should try to deny it. The denial can only be regarded as a symptom of ignorance or dishonesty.

It was quite late on Friday evening, May 18, when this Petition was finished and signed, and on Sunday morning, the 20th of May, the Royal Declaration had to be read in all the churches in London. There was therefore no time to be lost. Armed with their paper, six of the Seven Bishops (Sancroft being forbidden to come to Court) proceeded to Whitehall Palace, and had an interview with James II at 10 o'clock at night. The King took the Petition, and read it with mingled anger and amazement. He was both deeply displeased and astonished, and showed it. He never thought that English bishops would oppose his will. "I did not expect this," he said; "this is a standard of rebellion." In vain Trelawney fell on his knees, saying, "No Trelawney can be a rebel. Remember that my family has fought for the Crown." In vain Turner said, "We rebel? We are ready to die at your Majesty's feet." In vain Ken said, "I hope you will grant us that liberty of conscience which you grant to all mankind." It was all to no purpose. The King was thoroughly angry. "You are trumpeters of sedition," he exclaimed. "Go to your dioceses and see that I am obeyed." "We have two duties to perform," said noble Ken, "our duty to God and our duty to your Majesty. We honour you: but we fear God." The interview ended, and the bishops retired from the royal presence, Ken's last words being "God's will be done."

Before the sun rose on Saturday morning, May 19, the Bishops' Petition was printed, as a broadsheet, and hawked through all the streets of London. By whom this was done is not known to this day: but the printer is said to have made a thousand pounds by it in a few hours. The excitement was immense throughout the metropolis, and when Sunday came, next day, the churches were thronged with expecting crowds, wondering what the clergy would do, and whether they would read the King's Declaration. They were not left long in doubt. Out of one hundred parish Churches in the city and liberties of London, there were only four in which the Order in Council was obeyed, and in each case, as soon as the first words of the Declaration were uttered, the congregation rose as one man and left the Church.

At Westminster Abbey the scene was long remembered by the boys of Westminster school. As soon as Bishop Spratt, who was then Dean (a mean, servile prelate), began to read the Declaration, the murmurs and noise of the people crowding out completely drowned his voice. He trembled so that men saw the paper shake in his hand; and long before he had done, the Abbey was deserted by all but the choristers and the school. Timothy Hall, an infamous clergyman, who read the Declaration at St. Matthew's, Friday Street, was rewarded by the King with the vacant Bishopric of Oxford. But he bought his mitre very dear. Not one Canon of Christ Church attended his installation, and not one graduate would come to him for ordination.

A fortnight passed away, and on the 3rd of June the example of the London clergy was nobly followed in all parts of England. The Bishops of Norwich, Gloucester, Salisbury, Winchester, and Exeter, who were unable to reach London in time for the Lambeth Conference, had signed copies of the Petition, and, of course, refused to order obedience to the Declaration. The Bishop of Worcester declined to distribute it. In the great diocese of Chester, including all Lancashire, only three clergymen read it. In the huge diocese of Norwich, the stronghold of Protestantism, it was read in only four parishes out of twelve hundred. In short, it became evident that a spirit was awakened throughout the land which the Court had never expected, and that though the bishops and clergy might be broken, they would not bend.

Whether the King could break them remained yet to be proved. On the evening of the 8th of June, all the Seven Bishops, in obedience to a summons from the King, appeared before him in Council at Whitehall. They went provided with the best legal advice, and acted carefully upon it. They calmly refused to admit anything to criminate themselves, unless forced to do it by the King's express command. They were questioned and interrogated about the meaning of words in their Petition, but their answers were so guarded and judicious that the King gained nothing by the examination. They steadily held their ground, and would neither withdraw their Petition, nor confess they had done wrong, nor recede from their decision about the Declaration. At last they were informed that they would be prosecuted for libel in the Court of King's Bench, and refusing, by their lawyers' advice, to enter into recognizances for their appearance, they were formally committed to the Tower. A warrant was made out, and a boat was ordered to take them down the river.

Their committal to the Tower was the means of calling out an enthusiastic expression of feeling in London such as, perhaps, has never been equalled in the history of the metropolis. It was known from an early hour that the bishops were before the Council, and an anxious crowd had long waited round Whitehall to see what the result would be. But when the Londoners saw the seven aged prelates walking out of the palace under a guard of soldiers, and learned that they were going to prison (practically) in defence of English Protestantism, a scene of excitement ensued which almost baffles description. Hundreds crowded round them as they proceeded to Whitehall stairs, cheering them and expressing their sympathy. Many rushed into the mud and water up to their waists, blessing and asking their blessing. Scores of boats on the river full of people accompanied them down to the Tower with loud demonstrations of feeling. Even the very soldiers on guard in the Tower caught the infection and became zealous admirers of their prisoners. And when Sir E. Hales, the Popish governor, tried to check them, he was told by his subordinates that it was of no use, for his men "were all drinking the health of the bishops."

The seven prelates were kept in the Tower for a week. Throughout that time the enthusiastic feeling of admiration for them flared higher and higher, and increased more and more every day. They were almost idolized, as martyrs who had refused to truckle to a Popish tyrant, like Latimer and Ridley in Mary's days. The Church of England at one bound rose *cent per cent* in public estimation. Episcopacy was never so popular as it was that week. Crowds of people, including many of the nobility, went to the Tower every day to pay their respects to the venerable prisoners. Among them a deputation of ten leading Nonconformist ministers went to express their sympathy, and when the King sent for four of them and upbraided them, they boldly replied that they "thought it a solemn duty to forget past quarrels and stand by the men who stood by the Protestant cause." Even the Scotch Presbyterians were warmed and stirred in favour of the bishops, and sent messages of sympathy and encouragement. From every part of England came daily words of kindness and approbation. As for the men of Cornwall, they were so moved at the idea of their countryman, Trelawney, being in any danger, that a ballad was composed to suit the occasion, and sung over the county, of which the burden is still preserved.[80]

---

[80] The following is said to have been the ballad, but it is doubtful whether any part except the chorus is as old as 1688 :—
A good sword and a trusty hand,
A merry heart and true;
King James' men shall understand
What Cornish men can do!
And have they fixed the where and when,

And shall Trelawney die? And shall Trelawney die?
Then twenty thousand Cornish boys shall know the reason why.

Even the miners took up the song and sung it with a variation—

Then thirty thousand underground shall know the reason why.

A king of more common sense than James might well have been staggered by the astounding popularity of the seven episcopal prisoners, and would gladly have found some pretext for dropping further proceedings. But, unhappily for himself, he had not the wisdom to recede, and "drove on furiously," like Jehu (2 Kings 9:20), and drove to his own destruction. He decided to go on with the prosecution.

On the 15th of June the Seven Bishops were brought from the Tower to the Court of King's Bench, and ordered to plead to the information laid against them. Of course they pleaded "not guilty." That day fortnight, the 29th of June, was fixed for their trial, and in the meantime they were allowed to be at liberty on their own recognizances. It was well for the Crown that they did not require bail. Twenty-one peers of the highest rank were ready to give security, three for each defendant, and one of the richest Dissenters in the City had begged, as a special favour, that he

---

And shall Trelawney die?
Then twenty thousand Cornish men
Will know the reason why.

Chorus
And shall they scorn Tre, Pol, and Pen?
And shall Trelawney die?
Here's twenty thousand Cornish men
Will know the reason why.
Outspake their Captain, brave and bold—
A merry wight was he:
"If London Tower were Michael's Hold,
We'll set Trelawney free!
We'll cross the Tamar land to land,
The Severn is no stay,—
All side by side and hand to hand,
And who shall bid us nay?"

Chorus
And shall they scorn, etc.

might have the honour of being bail for Bishop Ken.

On leaving the court, in order to go to their own lodgings, the bishops received almost as great an ovation as when they were sent to the Tower. The bells of many churches were set ringing, and many of the lower orders who knew nothing of the forms of law imagined that all was over, and the good cause had triumphed. But whether ignorantly or intelligently, such a crowd assembled round the prelates in Palace Yard, that they found it difficult to force their way through their friends and admirers. Nor could it be said for a moment that the people knew not wherefore they were come together. One common feeling actuated the whole mass, and that feeling was abhorrence of Popery and zeal for Protestantism. How deep that feeling was is evidenced by a simple anecdote supplied by Macaulay:

> *Cartwright, Bishop of Chester, a timid sycophant of the Court, was silly and curious enough to mingle with the crowd as his noble-minded brethren came out of the Court. Some person who saw his episcopal dress supposed he was one of the accused, and asked and received his blessing. A bystander cried out, 'Do you know who blessed you?' 'Surely,' said the man, 'it was one of the seven.' 'No!' said the other, 'it was the Popish Bishop of Chester.' At once the enraged Londoner roared out, 'Popish dog, take your blessing back again.'*

At last, on the 29th of June, the ever-memorable trial of the Seven Bishops actually came off, and they were arraigned before a jury of their countrymen in the Court of King's Bench at Westminster. Such a crowd was probably never before or since seen in a court of law. Sixty peers according to Evelyn's diary, thirty-five according to Macaulay, sat near the four judges and testified their interest in the cause. Westminster Hall, Palace Yard, and all the streets adjoining were filled with a multitude of people wound up to the highest pitch of anxious expectation.

Into all the details of that well-fought day I cannot enter. How from morning till sunset the legal battle went on. How the Crown witnesses were cross-examined and worried. How triumphantly Somers, the fourth counsel of the bishops, showed that the alleged libel was neither false, nor libellous, nor seditious. How even the four judges were divided in opinion, and two of them went so far in their charge to the jury as to admit there was no libel. How the jury retired when it was dark to consider their verdict, and were shut up all night with the servants of the defendants sitting on the stairs to watch the doors and prevent roguery. How at length all the twelve jurymen were for acquittal except Arnold the King's brewer, and even he gave way when the biggest of the twelve said, "Look at me, I will stay here till I am no bigger than a tobacco pipe before I find the bishops guilty."

I cannot recount how at six in the morning the jury agreed, and at ten appeared in court, and by the mouth of their foreman, Sir Roger Langley, pronounced the bishops "Not Guilty." How at the words coming out of his lips Lord Halifax waved his hat, and at least ten thousand persons outside the court raised such a shout that the roof of old Westminster Hall seemed to crack. How the people in the streets caught up the cheer and passed it on all over London. How many seemed beside themselves with joy, and some laughed and some wept. How guns were fired and bells rung, and horsemen galloped off in all directions to tell the news of a victory over Popery. How the jury could scarcely get out of the Hall, and were forced to shake hands with hundreds crying out "God bless you, you have saved us all to-day." How when night came, bonfires were lighted and all London was illuminated and huge figures of the Pope were burnt in effigy.

All, all these things are so described in the burning words of Lord Macaulay's pictorial history that I shall not attempt to depict them. To go over the field so graphically occupied by that mighty "master of sentences" would be as foolish as to gild refined gold or paint the lily. Suffice it to say that the great battle of Protestantism against Popery was fought at this trial, that a great victory was won, and that to the prosecution and acquittal of the Seven Bishops James II owed the loss of his Crown.

For we must never forget that the consequences of the trial were enormously great, and that results flowed from it of which myriads never dreamed when they shouted and cheered on the 29th of June. Within twenty-four hours of the trial a letter left England for Holland, signed by seven leading Englishmen, inviting the Prince of Orange to come over with an army and overthrow the Stuart dynasty. The hour had come at last, and the man was wanted.

Within four weeks of the trial, Archbishop Sancroft, warmed and softened by the events of May and June, drew up a circular letter to all the bishops of the Church of England, which is one of the most remarkable letters ever penned by an Archbishop of Canterbury, and has never received the attention it deserves. In this letter he solemnly enjoined the bishops and clergy "to have a tender regard to our brethren the Protestant Dissenters, to visit them at their homes, to receive them kindly at their own, and to treat them fairly whenever they meet them." Above all, he charged them "to take all opportunities of assuring the Dissenters that the English bishops are really and sincerely irreconcilable enemies to the errors, superstitions, idolatries, and tyrannies of the Church of Rome." And, lastly, he urged them "to exhort Dissenters to join with us in fervent prayer to the God of peace for the universal blessed union of all reformed churches both at home and abroad." A wonderful pastoral that! Well would it have been for the Church of England if Lambeth had always held similar language, and not cooled down and forgotten the Tower. But it was one of the first results of the famous trial.

Last, but not least, within six months of the bishops' acquittal the Great Revolution took place, the Popish monarch lost his Crown and left England, and William and Mary were placed on the English throne. But before they were formally placed on the throne the famous "Declaration of Rights" was solemnly drawn up and signed by both Houses of Parliament. And what was the very first sentence of that Declaration? It is an assertion that "the late King James did endeavour to subvert and extirpate the Protestant religion—by assuming a power of dispensing with laws and by committing and prosecuting divers worthy prelates."

And what was the last sentence of the Declaration? It was the famous Oath of Supremacy, containing these words:—"I do declare that no foreign prince, person, prelate, state, or potentate hath, or ought to have, jurisdiction, power, superiority, pre-eminence, or authority, ecclesiastical or spiritual, within this realm. So help me God." Such were the immediate consequences of the trial of the Seven Bishops. They are of unspeakable importance. They stand out to my eyes in the landscape of English history, like Tabor in Palestine, and no Englishman ought ever to forget them. To the trial of the Seven Bishops we owe our second deliverance from Popery.

Practical lessons from this history

It remains for me to point out three practical lessons which appear to flow naturally out of the whole subject.

The Pope must not rule England

First and foremost, the reign of James II ought to teach a lesson about English rulers and statesmen, whether Whig or Tory. That lesson is the duty of never allowing the Government of this great country to be placed again in the hands of a Papist.

If this lesson does not stand out plainly on the face of history, like the handwriting at Belshazzar's feast, I am greatly mistaken. Unless we are men who having eyes see not, and having ears hear not, let us beware of Popish rulers. We know what they were in Queen Mary's days. We tried them a second time under James II. If we love our country, let us never try them again. They cannot possibly be honest, conscientious Papists if they do not labour incessantly to subvert English Protestantism, and turn everything upside down. I yield to no man in abhorrence of intolerance and religious persecution. I have not the slightest desire to put the clock back, and to revive such miserable disabilities as those of the Test and Corporation Acts. I am quite content with the Constitution as it is, and the laws which forbid the crown of England to be placed on the head of a Papist. But I hope we shall take care these laws are never repealed.

Some may think me an alarmist for saying such things. But I say plainly there is much in the outlook of the day to make a thinking man uncomfortable. I dislike the influence which certain well-known Roman Catholic divines are gradually getting among the upper classes. I dislike the growing disposition to make an idol of mere "earnestness," to forget history, and to suppose that Rome has changed, and earnest Papists are as good as any Protestant. I dislike the modern principle, unknown to the good old Puritans, that States have nothing to do with religion, and that it matters not whether the sovereign is Protestant or Papist, Jew, Turk, Infidel, or Heretic. I see these things floating in the air. I confess they make me uncomfortable.

I am sure we have need to stand on our guard, and to resolve that, God helping us, we will never allow the Pope to rule England again. If he does, we may depend upon it we shall have no more blessing from God. The offended God of the Bible will turn away his face from us, and we shall bid a long farewell to peace at home, influence abroad, comfort in our families, and national prosperity. Once more then, I say, let us move heaven and earth before we sanction a Popish prime minister or a Popish king. On the 28th January 1689, the House of Commons resolved unanimously "that it hath been found by experience inconsistent with the safety and welfare of this Protestant kingdom to be governed by a Popish prince."[81] I pray God that resolution may never be forgotten, and never be cancelled or expunged.

The strength of the Church is its Protestantism

In the second place, the reign of James II ought to teach us a lesson about English Bishops and Clergy. That lesson is the duty of never forgetting that the true strength of the Established Church of England lies in loyal faithfulness to Protestant principles and bold unflinching opposition to the Church of Rome.

Never was the Church of England so unpopular as in the days of Laud, and never so popular as in the days of the Seven Bishops. Never was the

---

81 Hallam, Volume 3, page 129.

Church so hated by Nonconformists as she was when Laud tampered with Rome, never so much beloved by them as when the Seven Bishops went to prison rather than help the Pope. Why was it that when Laud was committed to the Tower few hands were held up in his favour, and few said, "God bless him"? There is only one answer, men did not trust him, and thought him half a Papist.

Why was it that, when Sancroft and his companions were taken to the Tower fifty years afterwards, the heart of London was stirred, and the whole Metropolis rose up to do them honour? The answer again is simple. Men loved them and admired them because they stuck to Protestantism and opposed Rome.

Strive to maintain a confessionally-bound comprehensiveness

In the last place, the reign of James II ought to teach a lesson to all loyal Churchmen. That lesson is the duty of using every reasonable and lawful means to resist the re-introduction of Romanism into the Church of England by the means of extreme Ritualism.

It is useless to deny that the times demand this, and that there is an organized conspiracy among us for Romanizing the Established Church of this country. Bishops see it and lament it in their charges. Statesmen see it and make no secret of it in public speeches. Dissenters see it and point the finger of scorn. Romanists see it and rejoice. Foreign nations see it and lift up their hands in amazement. Whether this disgraceful apostasy is to prosper and succeed or not remains yet to be proved. But one thing, at any rate, is certain. This is no time to sit still, fold our arms, and go to sleep. The Church of England expects all her sons to do their duty, and much, under God, depends on the action of the laity.

It is false to say, as some of the advocates of extreme Ritualism constantly say, that those who oppose them want to narrow the limits of the Church of England, and to make it the exclusive Church of one party. I for one indignantly deny the charge. I have always allowed, and do allow, that our Church is largely comprehensive, and that there is room for honest High, honest Low, and honest Broad Churchmen within her pale. If any clergyman likes to preach in a surplice, or has the Lord's Supper weekly, or has Saints' day services, or daily matins and vespers, I have not the least wish to interfere with him, though I cannot see with his eyes. But I firmly maintain that the comprehensiveness of the Church has limits, and that those limits are the Thirty-Nine Articles and the Prayer-book.

Controversy and religious strife, no doubt, are odious things; but there are times when they are a positive necessity. Unity and peace are very delightful; but they are bought too dear if they are bought at the expense of truth. There is a vast amount of maundering, childish, weak talk nowadays in some quarters about unity and peace, which I cannot reconcile with the language of St. Paul. It is a pity, no doubt, that there should be so much controversy; but it is also a pity that human nature should be so bad as it is, and that the devil should be loose in the world. It was a pity that Arius taught error about Christ's person: but it would have been a greater pity if Athanasius had not opposed him. It was a pity Tetzel went about preaching up the Pope's indulgences: it would have been a far greater pity if Luther had not withstood him. Controversy, in fact, is one of the conditions under which truth in every age has to be defended and maintained, and it is nonsense to ignore it.

Of one thing I am very certain. Whether men will come forward or not to oppose the Romanizing movement of these days, if the Church of England once gives formal legal sanction to the revived Popish Mass and the revived detestable confessional, the people of this land will soon get rid of the Established Church of England. True to the mighty principles of the Reformation, our Church will stand and retain its hold on the affections of the country, and no weapon formed against us shall prosper. False to these principles, and re-admitting Popery, she will certainly fall, and no amount of histrionic, sensuous ceremonial will prevent her ruin. Like Ephesus, which left her first love,—like Thyatira, which suffered Jezebel to teach,—like Laodicea, which became lukewarm,—her candlestick will be taken away (Revelation 2-3). The glory will depart from her. The pillar of cloud and fire will be removed. The best and most loyal of her children will forsake her in disgust, and, like an army whose soldiers have gone away, leaving nothing behind but officers and band, the Church will perish, and perish deservedly, for want of Churchmen.

REFORMED FOUNDATIONS
REFORMING FUTURE
A Vision for 21st Century Anglicans

By Lee Gatiss & Peter Adam
Foreword by Bishop Wallace Benn

"A timely and important word... thoughtful, scholarly, and stimulating."
                        Christopher Ash

"A must read." Nigel Atkinson

"Stimulating and refreshing."
                    Archbishop Glenn Davies

This concise book explores the history, theology, and future of Anglicanism. Lee Gatiss unpacks the catholic, Protestant, and Reformed nature of the church's doctrine, and considers how it might apply today in questions of evangelical identity and arguments over women bishops.

Peter Adam goes on to unpack how Christ, as the sufficient and effective Saviour of his church, encourages us to engage faithfully in the ongoing ministry of reformation today.

These are edited versions of papers first delivered at the Church Society conference in 2013, which marked the 450th anniversary of the 39 Articles.

UK orders to Church Society: www.churchsociety.org
admin@churchsociety.org or call 01923 235111.
£5.00 each plus £1 postage; £22.00 for 5 copies; £40.00 for 10 copies.
Please add £2.00 postage for five or more copies.

Published by Lost Coin Books for Church Society
Paperback 73pages.
ISBN: 9781909559974

LOST C●IN

Church Society

CONFIDENT AND EQUIPPED
Facing Today's Challenges in the Church of England

Contributors: Lee Gatiss, Sam Allberry, Ben Cooper,
Simon Austen, John Richardson
Edited by Lee Gatiss

"A much needed blend of evangelistic passion, pastoral concern, and doctrinal conviction."   Vaughan Roberts

"Challenging, honest, engaging, realistic. Put this in the hands of as many as you can."   Hugh Palmer

"A timely and stimulating collection of papers for anyone thinking seriously about being a faithful evangelical in the Church of England today"   Christopher Ash

This concise book focuses on some of the key challenges facing those who seek to be faithful to the biblical gospel within the Church of England. It covers the significant pressure points of gender and same-sex attraction. But it also addresses the deeper long-term need to lead the way on evangelism within the structures of the denomination.

These stimulating chapters, edited versions of addresses first delivered at the Junior Anglican Evangelical Conference (JAEC) in September 2013, will help you to be both confident in the gospel, and equipped to face the challenges of remaining faithful in an increasingly hostile environment.

UK orders to Church Society: www.churchsociety.org
admin@churchsociety.org or call 01923 235111.
£5.00 each plus £1 postage; £22.00 for 5 copies; £40.00 for 10 copies.
Please add £2.00 postage for five or more copies.

LOST C●IN

Published by Lost Coin Books for Church Society
Paperback 108 pages.
ISBN: 9781910307076

Church Society

www.ingramcontent.com/pod-product-compliance
Lightning Source LLC
LaVergne TN
LVHW041617070426
835507LV00008B/297